This br
GRIEVE
in memory of Chris

MW00930018

Beautiful Grief

A Father and Daughter's
Brutally Honest Walk with Death

Katherine and Tony Rose

For speaking engagements and bulk purchases, contact:
Tony Rose
(818) 461-0600

Dedication

For Jonny Rose, who taught us as much through death as he did through life.

Acknowledgements

I want to thank all of my friends, but in particular, Brittany Cohen and Hayley Grossan, my college roommates, for always pushing me to grow and being my inspirations. Being your friend is empowering. To Erica, Krystal, Katie, and Melanie: Thank you for the constant support. You show up, always. And it never goes unnoticed.

I am also indebted to my mentors, Sean Stephenson and Jamie Del Fierro. Sean, thank you for pushing me toward my greatness. And Jamie, you allowed me to unearth strength and power I did not know I possessed.

And finally, to my mom and dad: Thank you for your support, for never giving up on me, and for showing me the power of love and loyalty. You embody the word "family."

—KR

I live in a state of appreciation for many. In no particular order (and fearful of omitting many), here goes:

Rebecca Snyder, you are an archangel of mercy and purpose. Greg Synder and the Turpins, Mark and Suzanne, thank you for expertly crafting Jon's memorial. Eric Swenson, you so graciously stepped in to moderate the event. Jon's God-family, the Berlins (Karen, Michael, Zach, and Molly), thank you for being our respite in a turbulent time.

The entire team at RSJ—Debbie Marks and Deborah Green, in particular—including all of my partners at RSJ, provided infinite support and tolerance.

Thank you, Jeffrey Lauterbach, for being the doorman to the liminal space.

My great friends and golf and fishing companions: Michael Gagan, Bret Morris, Gary Townsend, Domingo Such, Ian Hamel, Ron Stavert, and Kenny Stavert. You were a quiet presence who kept me looking at now and the future instead of the past. Kenny, your beautiful voice filled the Montana air in a tribute to my son and the friendship of our fishing buddies. That was spiritual ointment for a grieving spirit.

Jon's friends: You helped me realize more of the totality of who Jon was. Katie's friends: You walked this journey with Katie but also supported our entire family in a way you may never fully comprehend.

Katherine June Rose, your ageless wisdom made this book so much more than it could have been or what I ever thought it would be.

And finally, Chris: While you still suffer, you immediately understand that we did not die. You bore a burden no mother should ever bear, and yet, you did it without a single complaint. You are an example of perseverance for us all.

—TR

Only great writers and editors understand the difficulty of integrating two entirely different voices into one volume. Our friend and writer, Jocelyn Baker, is one of those writers. While every thought is ours, she honestly and with great care organized them so that this book could come to life. To her and of her, we are truly grateful and in total admiration.

—KR and TR

Table of Contents

The Loss of Everything

Justice failed and life succumbed

Outstripped of all things bright to come,

Now search for purpose lost at once

Nay breath it seems would be enough.

Youth betrayed to winter's end

Request of God our hearts to mend,

Our life's love lost, did God betray?

Since happiness seems far away,

Eventually we must decide, do we still live, or have we died?

—Bret Morris

Introduction

Tony

I met Liz—a pleasant, unassuming woman I guessed to be in her early forties—at a personal development conference called Human Information Technology. On the third morning of the conference, Liz stood and confided to our group of 63 people that each morning for the past 19 years, she awakened to thoughts of her son's death.

For 6,935 days, Liz's mind ran a loop that went something like this: Getting into the passenger side of her husband's car, buckling the belt over her pregnant belly, driving down her street, turning right, stopping for the young children who were playing in the road, her husband's nervous face as he watched the car behind him, which was not slowing down, feeling the impact of the 50-mile-per-hour crash as the car rear-ended her husband's car.

The doctor's words: "Your baby didn't make it."

Giving birth to her full-term dead son.

She had replayed the loop of her son's death so many times that it became automated.

What if we had waited five minutes? What if we had taken another route? What if...? What if...?

Yet, all of these *what ifs* led to this: Her son died before he could look into his mother's eyes. The loop was a labyrinth that led to the same place with no outlet other than devastation.

As you are sitting here reading this book and thinking of your own story of loss, you might find familiarity and even comfort in Liz's story. You are thinking, *Yes, yes, this is exactly how I feel. I am not alone.*

Even as you are comforted by knowing that there are others who understand your suffering, think forward to two weeks from now after you have finished this book. Consider that you might be able to create a new loop, a different script in your head that leads to somewhere other than devastation, and that over the coming months, you might even find happiness. You might take even greater comfort in realizing that you do have a future outside of the context of your current suffering and that this future begins today, as you start reading this book and finding ways to cut the loop in your own mind.

I think of my own wife, whom I married almost five decades ago, and who found the body of our own son, lifeless in his bed. I wonder if she wakes each morning and thinks about walking into his silent room, finding his motionless body, and trying to breathe life into her son. What a burden that must be. Yet, as I type these words, I know that we cannot live lives of *what ifs,* of *wouldas, couldas,* and *if onlys.*

We can only live with: What comes next?

Beautiful Grief began as a father-daughter project. Katie and I wanted to write this book together in part to create something tangible to represent our pain, our grief, and our healing, and in part to redefine our new relationship—one that now exists without Jonny, my son and Katie's brother. It was our "What comes next?"

Along the way, the project became much bigger. As we began talking to other people—people like Liz—we began to realize that our take on Jonny's death was inspirational.

Little did I understand, though, that Katie's profound words would also be an inspiration to me. When I started this project, I did not calculate how raw my own feelings were, nor did I realize how much Katie could help me heal. At the time, I thought my pain was well-sublimated.

I was wrong.

I had much healing yet to do. As I began reviewing Katie's writings within this book, I found myself confronted with pain that I had not yet processed. Her words comforted me, inspired me, and challenged me. I began to change. At times, I felt lighter. At times, I felt deeper. I was able to understand some of my pain in new terms, and I was able to enrich my grief—to allow it to inform and impact me.

I now see what Katie saw all along: We can all be inspired by the lessons from other people who have grieved. In this writing are seventeen of our learnings. Each chapter represents a different perspective—some from Katie and some from me—and from different timeframes in our journey. The final chapter summarizes these learnings, but I would suggest starting from the beginning. When you find a chapter that helps you deal with your grief, please share it with us on www.beautifulgrief.com.

Please also share your own learnings. What I now know, thanks to Katie, is that we can all help each other find beauty in our grief.

CHAPTER 1
JULY 27, 2015
TONY

"Jonny is dead."

These were the first words out of my wife's mouth. When I took her call, I was standing next to my friend Jeffrey Lauterbach in a golf bunker at Bandon Dunes Resort in North Bend, Oregon, learning how to hit balls from a sand trap.

At the time, Jeffrey was earning his Ph.D. in psychology, and he was in the early stages of writing his dissertation, titled *Golf in the Collective: Playing in the Liminal Space.*

Upon answering that devastating phone call, everything dropped away, and the sole matter in my mind was getting home to Chris, my wife of nearly five decades, and Katie, my then 23-year-old daughter, as quickly as possible.

Three years later, though, as I write these words, I am struck by the synchronicity of life and the timing of that phone call: As I began my own journey through the most challenging liminal space of my life, I happened to be standing next to a man writing his dissertation on that very topic.

At the time, I did not know what a "liminal space" was. Unless you have studied psychology, you likely do not either. Yet, as you sit reading this book, consider that your journey out of grief might begin right now, as you read the next few paragraphs and begin to understand the liminal space.

The word *liminal* comes from the Latin word *limen*, meaning "a threshold." It is the place wherein you have left one phase, one set of rituals or traditions, but you have not yet established new rituals. You no longer hold your pre-ritual status, but you have not yet begun to transition to a new status of rites and rituals. During the liminal stage, you are standing on the threshold between your previous way and what will become your new way.

To put it another way, where you are today, as well as who you are and what you are, is not where, or who, or what you were before you entered the liminal space. This you already know. A tsunami has hit your world.

Here is what you might not know: Where you are today, as well as who you are and what you are, is not where, or who, or what you are going to be after you travel through this space. It is natural for you to be here today, but you are in the process of being something new. It is as though you are taking a trip. You have left your hometown, and you have flown to a connecting airport, where you sit waiting to catch the flight to your destination.

The liminal space can seem permanent, and certainly so when grief accompanies it. Deep grief stems from the loss of a relationship or an extreme shift in conditions that changes the dynamic and balance in such a profound way that the circumstances of joy that persisted before the liminal phase cannot be recaptured.

This loss can seem enduring. After all, how can you be okay when the joy you once had can never again be realized?

Yet, the liminal space need not be permanent. You can come out of it, and you can eventually see a future of happiness and joy. Your pain does not need to shackle you.

The matter of *how* you come out of it is the subject of this book, and the short answer is this: You begin to transition out of the liminal space when the future becomes a larger conversation than your past.

We all travel through the liminal space at various times in life. We see couples enter the liminal space when they become newlyweds, navigating the waters of living together. They enter the liminal space again when they become parents and again when they become empty nesters.

Throughout our lives, most of us transition from elementary school to middle school, from child to adult, from student to employee, from single to married (and perhaps to divorced), from one house to another house, from one city to another.

From with Jonny to without Jonny.

Sometimes, the liminal space lasts a moment, a day, or years. Some people enter the liminal space and never exit, their world getting snagged in a Twilight Zone of sorts. Those around them, and the world, move on, but they teeter on a precipice, unable to step back and not wanting to step forward.

The beginning of my liminal journey happened on that golf course. The moment I answered Chris's incoming phone call, I entered a transitional phase that I have now begun to exit. Jonny's death left a hole in my heart that will never close, but I am also growing because of that hole. At times, I am even hopeful. My family dynamics have changed, but we are perhaps more resilient. Yet, much is yet to be determined. I am being redefined as a man with a dead son, and I am finding my place in the world within the context of this new definition.

Katie's journey would begin several minutes later when Chris made that same devastating phone call to our youngest child, who was working at her new job.

And Chris's journey had already begun. When she called me in the late afternoon from our kitchen in Sherman Oaks, she had already discovered Jonny's body in his bed in our pool house, his cell phone still in hand. She had already called 911. Already put her own lips to her 28-year-old son's mouth in a powerless attempt to resuscitate him.

Over the course of the next ten hours, I traveled home, alone with my thoughts—first by limousine from the golf resort to the airport in North Bend, Oregon; then by 12-passenger commuter plane from North Bend to Portland; and, finally, to Los Angeles, where I caught a cab home.

I am sure that I interacted with the limousine driver, the pilots, the airline attendants, and the taxi driver. I remember wanting to tell everyone that my son had died. As I walked through security, boarded the plane, and spoke to the flight attendant, I wanted to share in the enormity of my loss. It seemed absurd to tell the flight attendant that I wanted peanuts rather than pretzels without also letting her know that my son had died.

For the most part, though, I remember feeling relieved that I could be quiet with myself. I was absent the details of Jonny's death, and I cycled through all of the possible scenarios. Had he committed suicide? Had he overdosed? How long had he been dead? Had it been painful? What horrors must Chris have endured?

I was also given the gift of having time to reflect on what I could give to Chris and Katie. How would I show up? What would I say? I am certain that had I not been granted those ten hours of time alone, I would not have been able to respond in the way that I did.

When I arrived home at 2 a.m., I was greeted by an amazing site: Our loved ones had quietly formed a circle of chairs in my driveway. Jonny's dear friends Alex and Dennis, Katie's dear friends Erica and Katie, and many others sat with my wife, holding her hand, smoking and drinking with her, and everyone keeping each other upright. If you can imagine, picture yourself driving up in a taxi, the floodlights illuminating chairs where people you love are arrayed in a circle. It was strangely wonderful, like floating on mattress of love and support.

My first words to Chris were, "This is going to change our lives, but we cannot let this ruin us."

• • •

This past year, on the three-year anniversary of Jonny's death, I was traveling home from a business trip. My plane would not land back in Los Angeles until the late afternoon, which meant my wife would be alone on the anniversary of our oldest child's death. I asked Chris if she wanted me to change my itinerary so that I could be with her earlier in the day.

"Why?" she asked. "Jonny doesn't die again on July 27, 2018."

When she spoke those words, I knew that Chris, too, had started to leave the liminal space, forming a new life ahead of her.

As you read this book, know that being in the liminal space is natural. To be sure, when liminal space is accompanied by grief, it feels dark and all-encompassing. This is normal. What you have is not an incurable sickness. You are not tragic and beyond hope for feeling as though your life is over. After all, in a way, your life as you knew it is over.

Yet, the liminal space is a moment, a period of time. It is not forever. Instead, it is a time marked by choice. What do you do next? Do you remain shackled in grief, or do you find a victory over—and even a companionship with—grief?

This book does not have all of the answers. Katie and I share our most intimate thoughts—sometimes dark and shameful but often determined and optimistic—as we journey out of the liminal space. But most of all, we hope to give you one click. If we can move you just one click in the direction of exiting the liminal space, we have done our job.

CHAPTER 2
WHAT THE HELL JUST HAPPENED?
KATIE

You would think that when the apocalypse comes, people would stop calling restaurants to make dinner reservations.

That is not what happens, though. When your whole world falls apart, the rest of the world keeps on going on. In the blink of an eye, you find yourself neck-deep in a liminal space. It is as though your whole world has been flipped upside down and has frozen in time, yet the outside world fails to notice. The phone keeps ringing. You still need to go to the grocery store to buy dog food. You still have to listen to other people's menial conversations.

If you happen to be across town at work when you learn that your brother dies, you would think that traffic would open up. It does not, though. You still have to sit through 45 minutes of stop-and-go traffic, red lights, and rude Los Angeleno drivers while you fight your way home to be with your mom.

Your mom. You will be unable to stop thinking about your mom. What must it have been like for your mom to find her oldest child dead in his bed?

"What the hell? What the hell?" you will think through tears, sobbing in the car, and biting your hand to try to stay in control. You still have to drive. You still have to stay between the yellow lanes. You still have to wait your turn at stop signs.

Suicide? Overdose? What in the world killed your 28-year-old brother? Was it related to his seizure?

Six months before Jonny died, he had a seizure at work. Jonny had been hired by a prominent law firm shortly after graduating from law school and passing the bar, and I think he assumed that a six-figure income was right around the corner. Knowing Jonny, he probably thought he would charm his way to partner within minutes. I am sure that "have a seizure while at my new job" was not high on his list, but that is what happened.

He collapsed on the damn floor.

I happened to be pulling into my dad's office right after he got the call from Jonny's boss saying that Jonny was being taken to the hospital. My dad jumped in my car, and we raced to the hospital, arriving just as the ambulance pulled up. Jonny was pulled out of the ambulance feet-first. I did not need to see anything else: I knew my brother by his ugly-ass lime green shoes.

When we saw his face, Jonny was pale but conscious. He shrugged, as if to say, "What the hell just happened?"

Jonny's doctors could not explain his seizure. Brain scans showed nothing abnormal that would point toward epilepsy. At the time, his toxicology report was clean. It was a medical mystery, but one thing was certain: Jonny could not safely operate a vehicle until he had six months seizure-free. His license was suspended.

Fortunately for Jonny, I happened to be fresh out of college, and, at that point, without a job. After his seizure, I became Jonny's chauffeur. For 45 minutes every morning and every evening, I drove Jonny to and from work. We listened to rap music. We talked about our future plans. And we talked about Ally, the woman he had started dating.

Their first date was at a restaurant in West Hollywood. I remember that Jonny wore too much cologne and his ugly-as-sin lime green shoes. Apparently, Ally did not mind.

It was Ally who called me on the day Jonny died. It was about 3 p.m., and Ally had not heard from Jonny. By that time, they had been dating seven months and were connected at the hip. He texted her first thing in the morning and last thing at night. When she had not heard from him by late afternoon, she called me to see if he was okay.

By then, Jonny had lost his job. (Suffice it to say, he never did charm his way to partner.) I, on the other hand, had found a job, and I was working when Ally called. I was not particularly concerned. By that time, Jonny was in a funk: Being laid off had been a giant blow to his self-esteem. I had never before seen Jonny as depressed as he was in the weeks and months before he died. Six months earlier, Jonny thought he was on his to a six-figure income and a partnership. Instead, he was unemployed and living in his parents' pool house.

Sometimes, Jonny did not emerge until 5 p.m.

Nonetheless, I called my mom to see if she had heard from Jonny. My mom works in the library of a private school, so on July 27, 2015, she was home on summer break.

"Have you seen Jonny?" I asked.

"No," said my mom.

"Ally has not heard from him, and she is worried. Can you go check on him?"

"Sure."

"Okay. I have to get off the phone," I said. My new employer was a restaurant with a romantic atmosphere and a pricey menu. My instructions from the start had been clear: When working in the office, do not, under any circumstances, let a call go to voicemail.

"Text me and let me know that everything is okay," I said before returning to my job.

I knew something was wrong when my mom did not immediately text me to let me know that Jonny was okay. Twenty minutes later, my cell phone buzzed. I felt relief to see my mom's name on the screen, sure that she was calling to tell me that Jonny was hungover but otherwise fine.

"Jonny is dead," she said, speaking the same words she had said to my father just minutes earlier. "Jonny is dead. You need to come home."

That was it. She hung up.

And yet, the world kept turning. The office phone rang, and I answered it.

"Good afternoon. This is Katie. Can I help you?" I spoke those words, and I listened to the other person. Maybe I took a reservation. Maybe I talked to a vendor. Maybe it was a wrong number. I was in shock, but I played the part.

My brother was dead, and I was supposed to keep answering the damn phone.

When I could breathe, I called Diane, a co-worker who was working at our other restaurant in West Hollywood.

"My brother died, and I need to go home," I said. "I do not know who will answer the phones if I leave."

Everything was surreal: The severity of my brother's death had not sunk in. My parents were going to attend their first-born's funeral. We would have to decide whether to cremate his body.

These thoughts were not on my mind. Just, *who will answer the phones?*

"Go home," said Diane. "I do not know why you are still there. Stop worrying about the phones. Go."

After I got in my car, I kicked into gear. I called my godmother and told her to get to my house immediately. My mom could not be alone. I called my best friends, and as reality began setting in, I started to hyperventilate. I do not remember making my way from the crowded streets of Santa Monica onto the 405 Freeway, merging onto the 101 at the beginning of rush hour traffic, but I remember biting my hand because I was getting lightheaded and I knew I had to calm my breathing so that I could make it home safely.

When I arrived in front of my house, I jumped out of my car without pulling it to the curb. One of my dad's partners, Rebecca, was walking into my house at the same time. Someone must have parked my car for me. Maybe it was Rebecca.

In a crisis, those small obstacles stop having any weight at all. Whatever it is—death or divorce or disease, or something else entirely—when it is big, everything else seems unimportant. You can look at the rest of the world, operating as usual, and you can see how ridiculous it looks. Parking your car in an orderly fashion? Why the hell does it matter? How is there a world in which people are dying, and yet, we are expected to park within six to eighteen inches of the curb? If you have lost something, you know that feeling—that feeling of hovering outside the world, no longer really a part of it, and being able to see every triviality with perfect clarity.

It was helpful for me to name that time—to call it "the liminal space" so that I could put words to what was happening. I felt disconnected, as if I no longer belonged in the world. Knowing that this feeling was shared by other people—that there was a name for the bizarre world I found myself thrust into—gave me a sense of normalcy when nothing else seemed the same.

The ambulance was gone by the time I arrived home. I ran inside and found my mom in the kitchen, along with police officers. Did you know that police officers will come to your house if someone dies? Such was my good fortune to have never had that knowledge earlier.

Why was Jonny dead? It was all a blur. Friends walked in, and we ran to each other and held each other. Someone offered me water. Someone else made food. A friend of mine who had been in another city suddenly arrived, as though she had teleported to Los Angeles. Someone put something in the microwave. A friend washed a dish. None of it made any damn sense. Just, *what the hell is happening?*

Then came the coroner, standing in my kitchen. I remember thinking: *Pay attention, Katie. This seems important.* But it was just more background noise.

"I am going to take the body now," he said. "You will get a toxicology report in four weeks. Do you have any questions?"

Yes.

Am I an only child now?

CHAPTER 3
THAT DAMN BOX
KATIE

My brother's ashes are stored inside a box.

To be completely accurate, they are not ashes at all. When a person's body is cremated, everything is incinerated except bone matter, which is ground into a fine powder that looks like ashes, then poured into an urn.

If I am being precise, then, my brother's *bone fragments* are stored inside a damn box. You can probably see the irony of putting a person inside a box, whether it is an urn or a casket. After all, if we learn anything from death, it is this: People are too divergent, too unconstrained, to be put inside a box. Try as you might, you cannot hold all of the pieces of a person in one place. They will spill out. Just when you think you have captured a person, you will notice something on the other side of the room that does not fit.

The stories that come pouring in after a person dies are meant to comfort you, and perhaps they will, but they will also shock the hell out of you. You will learn all sorts of new information—proof that your dead brother, your dead spouse, your dead friend, or your dead child had dimensions to their personality that you never knew existed.

If you are their sister, maybe you knew that their childhood room was disgusting. Or you knew about the fights they had with their parents and their girlfriends. You knew the story about the time they went on a family trip to Hawaii and got drunk on the beach while they were supposed to be in the hotel room sleeping.

You can probably recite the collection of shared family memories, but here is the thing: You will find that you are unable to define the whole person with clear, contained boundaries. As those stories come pouring in, you might think: *I did not know this person at all.*

The reality is that you knew only ten or fifteen percent, and it probably was not the ten or fifteen percent that the rest of the world knew.

I know many things about Jonny, some of which no one else in the world knows, and yet, I cannot tell you who Jonny was with absolute certainty. I cannot put him inside any one box. If you forced me to describe him to you, I would say this: My brother was a raging asshole to me, and he was the embodiment of a hail-fellow-well-met to everyone else. He was a superstar in high school and college, and he was, at best, mediocre in law school. He was a great teammate. He was charming, kind, and welcoming of people. He was a terrible big brother. He was a great employee whose coworkers loved him, but whose boss laid him off. He was a loving boyfriend. His girlfriend believed that *they* would marry, and his ex-girlfriend believed that *they* would eventually marry. He was angry and hurt and broken, and he was the sort of person who could heal other people with a smile.

At the end of the day, he was all of these things. In a lot of ways, these things do not add up, but they are true nonetheless. He was, as the saying goes, a riddle wrapped in a mystery inside an enigma.

The stories that I heard about Jonny all painted this picture of him as a sparkling, shining beacon of friendliness and goodness—the kind of guy who never met a stranger.

Yet, I never got to meet that person. In the 23 years that my brother shared with me, I have few memories of Jonny speaking a kind word to me. He yelled at me, threatened me, and mocked me. I begged him for compassion, and he gave me none.

After he died, Jonny's friend Alex said, "He was pretty fucking close to not having a bad bone in his body." But, at times, I was not sure Jonny had anything but bad bones in his body. Whereas his friends got love, I got hate and vitriol. The Jonny I saw was nothing like the Jonny that Alex and Jake and Cash and Dennis and Dustin and Ally and Sam saw. For every story they have of Jonny's hospitality, I have two of his rage. Some of them—like the time he screamed at me because I refused to help him make a drug deal in Las Vegas—were not witnessed by anyone else, but they still happened. My stories do not reconcile with other people's stories, but they were still part of Jonny, part of his character, part of his history.

I never witnessed the ten or fifteen percent of Jonny that shined. I got the lousiest parts of him.

Who is right, then? If all of his friends are painting him as charming and gregarious—nearly angelic—what does that make me? Am I a liar? Overly sensitive?

I assure you that I am not.

But, if I paint him as an asshole, what does that mean to all of you who loved him? Am I destroying the box that you built—the one with four walls containing Jonny as a purely benevolent human being?

Trying to make sense of a person, of the details of their life, of the moments proceeding their death, can drive you mad. You can rehash it over and over, hoping to find a reasonable explanation. *Why did my brother hate me? No, he did not hate me; he was broken. Then why did he act like he hated me? Was I undeserving of his love? He did love you; he just did not know how to say it. But he said it to everyone else. Is something wrong with me?*

The rumination can begin to consume you.

You know what, though? If you cannot put someone else inside a box, you can't put yourself inside a box either. Take me, for instance. I would give anything to spend another day with Jonny, even if he were abusing me. I am also glad that Jonny is dead because I do not have to put up with his meanness anymore. I am distraught for the relationship that will never be, and I feel so damn relieved that I do not have to navigate the relationship we had.

All of those things are true, and depending on the day and my mood, they move to the foreground or the background. I am afraid I am just not that simple either. My emotions are not well-ordered or tied together with a ribbon.

I am coming to realize that they may never be.

Human beings are mysterious and open for interpretation. They shift, they grow, they break. They say things they do not mean. They do not say things they wish they said. Sometimes, they hide, and sometimes, they put on a brave face. Those of us on the receiving end never really know for sure what is real, what is amplified, and what is hidden. There are too many variables. *Was Jonny going through something? Was there something I just did not see? Was he slowly changing, shifting shapes, and becoming a different version of himself?*

Yes, to all of that.

And I will simply have to come to terms with the fact that I will never know the answers to my question for sure. I will never get the answers I want. It is out of the question. Jonny is not here to answer.

The best we can do, then, is to allow the questions to remain unanswered, and to make our own meaning instead. Absent answers to our questions, we have to interpret the past—whatever it is—in the way that best allows us to live powerfully and joyfully in the present and in the future. Since we cannot know for certain, we must do the best we can.

And if you think about it, being unable to put someone inside a box opens up a certain freedom. For me, it means finding compassion for a brother who saved the best for his friends while giving the worst to me. The strongest way that I can interpret all those unanswered questions is to say that it was an honor to bear witness to the worst of a person. People show their rawest sides to the people they love most and who cannot leave them. I saw the side of Jonny that was broken. He could show it to me because I was his sister. The risk of losing me was nonexistent. He could say horrible things to me, and I would show right back up, ready to watch him from the bleachers or drive him around for five months, eager to share something—anything—positive.

Jonny gave everything he had to the outside world, and when he came home, he had nothing left to give to me. He was probably clinically depressed, and he had to give this pain to someone. He showed me his box of secrets that he hid from the rest of the world.

I tell myself this: Other siblings go on to resolve their conflicts, to look back and laugh about the years of fighting. Given time, Jonny and I would have resolved our sibling rivalry and grown into adults who were close. Jonny gave me everything that he could offer me at the time, given the tools that he had and the pain he was suffering. Those months of driving Jonny to and from work created peace within Jonny with respect to our relationship so that he could transition from this world into the spirit world.

Is that true? I do not know; I cannot know. Does it matter? If believing this version of the story helps me move forward, do we really need to argue about whether my version of Jonny was right, or whether Alex's or my mom's or my dad's version of Jonny was right? My brother was finding himself, sorting through pain and failure to decide what kind of man he was going to become. I will only know a small sliver of that Jonny, just the ten or fifteen percent of him that was angry and hurt and broken, but there was more to him that he would have shown me and more that he would have become, eventually.

The people who have died—they are not here to tell you that you are right or that you are wrong. You get to decide what was real, what was authentic, and what was true. You will never know for sure. You will never know the real story of anyone, or even if there is a real story. The only thing you can force inside a box are bone fragments. The rest? Let it spill out.

CHAPTER 4
MOMENT STACKING
TONY

These are the two options as I have come to see them: First, I can let the loss of Jonny define my life, attaching sorrow to every interaction. Certainly, this option can be tempting. The grief, at times, has been numbing.

If this is the option I choose, the act of grieving will become the holy ritual. The event that created my transition into the liminal space will become the outcome in my life. I will write a book *because* my son died. I will cry at coming-of-age stories *because* my son died. I will lose weight *because* my son died.

The other option is this: I can feel the loss of my son while continuing to make all efforts to make my future better than my past. My son's death can be an "and" in my life, not a "because." I am writing a book... *and* my son died. I cry at coming-of-age stories... *and* my son died. I lost weight... *and* my son died.

For most people who are grieving the loss of a loved one, this option can feel close to impossible.

So, exactly *how* is it done?

In my case, it began with a chair and ended with a wedding dance.

The Chair

On the eve of the first Thanksgiving without my son, I found myself fixated on thoughts of who would sit in Jonny's chair. For as long as I could remember, my family sat in this arrangement: I sat at the head, Katie was at the foot, Jonny to her immediate right, and Chris to my immediate right. Almost always, others joined us for the more formal family meals, but regardless, we seemed to gravitate toward those seats. I cannot tell you how that seating arrangement began. It certainly was not something we deliberated on as a family. It occurred organically, without notice.

As Thanksgiving approached four months after Jonny's death, I found myself consumed with thoughts of his chair. Chris, Katie, and I hosted Thanksgiving, and we invited a few friends and family members. It felt impossible to simultaneously grieve and feel thankful, as one is supposed to do on Thanksgiving, yet we were determined to go through the motions.

But I could not wrap my head around the answer to the question of who would sit in Jonny's chair, nor could I wrap my feelings around it. I fluctuated between feeling numb and feeling overwhelmed with grief.

Would someone sit in his chair, or would it sit empty, a loud vacancy reminding us that someone was missing? An insignificant, modest chair, one that just six months earlier would never have owned a piece of my energy, was suddenly consuming my thoughts.

That's the funny thing about rituals and traditions: We might not notice the ones we celebrate the most until they cease to exist. Of course, the once-in-a-blue-moon rituals like our own weddings and the funerals of our loved ones hit with a splash, but the daily rituals—the ones like driving the same path to work or always checking the mailbox on the way into the house after work or sitting in the same chair—take little to no conscious space in our minds. They simply exist.

Until they do not.

And when they do not, the absence of the ritual is a scream. WHO WILL SIT IN THE CHAIR?

These are the moments when Jonny's absence makes the world seem bleak. The void left by Jonny's death was felt that evening, and that damn chair was a symbol of grief. Everyone who attended that Thanksgiving meal knew where Jonny should have been sitting.

If we did not fill that chair with a body, Thanksgiving would have been a *because,* meaning this: "We are in mourning this Thanksgiving *because* my son died." We could have left the chair empty, and we would have remembered that void forever, a reminder that Jonny would never sit in that chair.

To do so, though, would have sentenced us to letting that empty chair define our lives, the result of which would have been that our thoughts were so focused on what we did *not* have that we would have missed the moments of joy available to us.

If we permitted that chair to be filled with something new, on the other hand, with a different body, we would also permit a new moment, a new kind of Thanksgiving. We would permit the day to unfold as an *and.* "We are celebrating Thanksgiving dinner... *and* my son died."

When we allow someone to sit in the chair, we open up the possibility of a moment of joy, which stacks onto another moment of joy, which stacks onto another moment of joy, which begins to turn not into a moment, but into a day, and then into a life.

I call this "moment stacking," and what it means is that I allow for new moments to accumulate, moments that exist without Jonny. When I pile enough of them on top of one another into a new stack of moments, I can create those new rituals. I can cross through the liminal space into a life that exists without Jonny. My moments with Jonny still exist, but new stacks of moments have accumulated beside them.

It helps me to visualize these moment stacks as separate entities. The stack of moments that included Jonny is complete. It will never be erased, but it will not have new layers. I do not allow the moments that I had with Jonny to be the organ that pumps into the moments that I have now. If everything is in the same stack—if I try to pile new moments atop the moments I shared with Jonny—then my life becomes a *because*. Everything that happens is in the context of Jonny, and it is directed by what lies beneath it. My future becomes fed primarily by my moments with Jonny. Jonny's memories become the lifeblood of everything I have in the future.

I do not wish for this to be the case.

I want Jonny's memories to exist, but I want them to exist as a complement to new moments. I want them to enrich me but not to take me over. The closest I can come to explaining this is to tell you about the wedding I attended in January of 2018.

The Wedding

I was honored to be a guest at my employee Carmen's wedding to Fernando. Carmen manages our administrative staff, and she has remained one of the most articulate, calm, and steadfast employees our firm has ever had the great fortune of hiring. She has worked for the firm for about six years, and she has always surprised me with her depth and her purposefulness.

But to be honest, before Carmen's wedding, her fiancé was an acquaintance. He and I had met a handful of times prior to the wedding. We had exchanged pleasantries and small talk. I liked him, and I was pleased for Carmen, whom I respect and cherish as a person and as an employee. Had Jonny not died, though, I am certain that his wedding to Carmen (which marked their own liminal journey, albeit a more joyful one) would not have been as extraordinary as it ended up being for me.

Yet, I can say without a doubt that I will never forget watching Fernando dance with his mother on his wedding day. I found myself crying, watching a mother so tenderly celebrate the love and happiness she felt for her adult son, mixed with the bittersweet emotion of seeing her baby turn into a man, which was, by the way, also a liminal journey. I watched them dancing, aware that I will never have a memory of Jonny dancing with his own mother but sure that I would never have otherwise recognized the beauty and the quiet confluence of melancholy and joy. It was—even as I think about it now—a moment that will always move me. There's no question in my mind that it was almost as consequential as Jonny's birth itself.

I will remember Fernando dancing with his mother until my dying day. I can, at this very instant, see a picture of them dancing in my mind.

As I watched them, it occurred to me that those empty places that I thought would never be filled can be filled if I let them. Watching Fernando dance with his own mother did not have to be a reminder of what I did not have: It was better as a great substitute, a beautiful replacement for a hole that would otherwise be vacant, a small, surprising moment I could treasure in my mind as its own memory.

This is the closest I have come to being grateful for the context given to me by Jonny's death. It was the first time I really articulated that there would be many glorious moments to come. I began to realize that the moments did not have to come from Chris, or from Katie, or from me, or even from someone in my immediate circle—they could come from an acquaintance. I could share in a moment with my employee's fiancé and his mother—a moment that he will never forget, but equally, a moment that I will never forget.

I could have thought, *Jonny will never dance with his mom*, and I would have missed the moment between Fernando and his mother. Instead, I was able to share in a beautiful moment between Fernando, Carmen, and their families. Absent the context of Jonny's death, I would have been an attendee at Fernando and Carmen's wedding. Given the context of Jonny's death, I was a participant. The world, and all of the moments that unfolded at that wedding, seemed so much richer, with more depth of color, than I could have otherwise seen them. I am certain that Jonny's death has made me a better person who is more capable of experiencing life.

The stack of moments that I had with Jonny, including the memories and lessons of his death, certainly expanded the amount of sadness I had ever felt, but in doing so, my entire emotional bandwidth was stretched. Joy, happiness, love, compassion: I am convinced that the extent to which you can feel them is directly proportional to the amount of pain, grief, sadness, and devastation you have felt.

While I never would have chosen for my son to die, I intend to extract every bit of wonder, wisdom, and joy that I can from the experience. I intend to watch the dances, to invite people in, to see what happens when life is an *and*.

• • •

And yes, I intend to let people sit in chairs, which is what happened on that Thanksgiving Day. Jonny's dearest childhood friend sat in his chair, and the day unfolded so naturally that today, I am aware of who sat in that chair only because Katie reminded me. Instead, my memory is filled with the feelings of love and support I felt on that day. I am sure that if we had preserved Jonny's chair, these memories would never have solidified to later shine through. Instead, I would remember the empty chair.

This is the push and pull of his death. We have a choice—look backward and spend our time bemoaning what we no longer have or look forward and hold open the moments of life that will unfold. Even in the context of death and grief, we can stack moments, allowing them to pile up so that, like rocks piling on one side of a teeter totter, the balance begins to shift in the direction of happiness.

If you are in the enviable position of having never lost someone whose presence has been a constant, what you may not have considered is this: Is it appropriate to imagine a future with joy? Is it appropriate to say, "My son is dead... *and* some of my best moments are still ahead of me"?

Can these things coexist? I believe so.

Someday, I will laugh so hard that my side hurts. I will feel a joy that I never imagined possible. And my son is dead.

CHAPTER 5
STOP CRYING
KATIE

Jonny's funeral was held in Burbank, a suburb of Los Angeles, at Lakeside Golf Club. Like most golf clubs, Lakeside hosts weddings and other gatherings, and, apparently, funerals. To give you some idea of how large Jonny's funeral was, Lakeside could not accommodate all the cars. People had to park in the streets and walk a quarter of a mile. We live-streamed the service into an overflow room because the main ballroom could not seat everyone.

I do not know the exact headcount, but I am guessing that Jonny's funeral was attended by well over 500 people, including his friends from elementary school, high school, college, law school, his hockey and lacrosse teams, his internships, and his jobs. More than a few of my friends were there, as well as my mom and dad's friends, clients, and colleagues.

My dad was horrified because, when I stood up to speak about my relationship with Jonny and my memories of him, I dropped an f-bomb.

In my defense, it seemed fitting: My brother had died five days earlier. No one should have to go through that. Besides, we were there to honor Jonny. It is not like he had the cleanest mouth in the world, so I said "fuck" in front of my dad's employees and clients.

I guess that when your brother dies, it feels messed up no matter what, even if you know it is coming, but I kept thinking about how sudden and unexpected Jonny's death was. I wish I had some concrete warning so that I could have been psychologically prepared. I certainly did not think that, at the age of 23, I would be spending my summer planning and attending my brother's funeral, so it is no wonder that so many people appeared to support our family. I hope that my crassness did not offend any of them. My entire world was collapsing. I was not thinking clearly, and I was fucking distraught. I apologize.

Looking back, it strikes me that his funeral was the first time that a room of Jonny's loved ones would convene without him, but it would not be the last time.

There have been holidays and weddings that Jonny could not attend, and there will be more in the future. If I have children, he will not celebrate the birth of those children. He will not post pictures of his newborn nieces and nephews on his social media sites—the proud uncle holding a six-pound baby. There will be embarrassing moments I want to share when the only person who would make me laugh is dead.

When my parents celebrate their fifty-year anniversary, many of the people who attended Jonny's funeral will be in the room, but Jonny will not be there. Will those moments always feel empty and sad when I realize that Jonny is not part of them?

In any death, a funeral is a formal announcement: Never would that group of people otherwise convene, and yet the glue—the person bringing them together—is absent. It is the first moment, the first realization that the person who *is supposed to be there* is not there. The lack of the person's physical body at his or her funeral is palpable. The funeral marks the end of a life and the beginning of a world of people and events that will continue living nonetheless, no matter how stunned and ill-prepared they might be as they stand in that room, together but feeling so disconnected from the world.

And, to be clear, Jonny's was not a quiet presence. When we convened for his funeral, we were not mourning the loss of a person who otherwise faded into the background. Jonny was noticeable. Gregarious, loud, and funny, at least on the surface, he had an enthusiastic, contagious laugh, and he welcomed everyone.

Have you ever arrived at a party only to realize you did not know anyone? Jonny was that guy who brought you into the crowd. During those first days of Jonny's death, I was struck by how many people said that Jonny was the first friend they had—the "first friend" on the hockey team, the "first friend" in the classroom, the "first friend" at college, the "first friend" at work.

After Jonny's funeral, one of his first friends, Alex, shared a story with me that perfectly sums up Jonny's relationship with the outside world.

Jonny met Alex when they were just six or seven at coach-pitch Little League. A few years later, they started playing roller hockey in a parking lot, and they would eventually play on a travel hockey team together. Later, they went to the same high school.

In other words, Alex and Jonny were tight. They had that friendship that comes with two decades of aggregated experience. When you read this story, I want you to imagine this: your best friend, with a lifetime of love between you, easy to share a laugh. *That's* the friendship Jonny and Alex shared.

The story goes like this: Jonny and Alex were walking down the street when Jonny spotted a fire hydrant. It was just your typical fire hydrant, but the guys were not exactly sober, and boy did Jonny love to laugh. Because of the two plugs sticking out from the side of the hydrant, they decided it looked like a person.

What did Jonny do? He put his Red Sox hat on top of the fire hydrant and offered it a beer. Naturally, Jonny wanted the fire hydrant to feel at home.

Alex, of course, was on the floor laughing in that side-splitting way that you best friend can make you laugh. That's when Jonny pulled out a Marlboro Light and offered the fire hydrant a cigarette.

Remember what Alex said about Jonny? "He was pretty fucking close to not having a bad bone in his body." Those were Alex's words when he told me this story.

And Alex wasn't the only one. Everyone said the same things about Jonny: Always the social butterfly, he was the guy who remembered not only everyone's names but also their dreams and fears. Jonny was the always-hospitable friend who noticed when a person was sad or uncomfortable and who did what he could to alleviate the discomfort. He was the guy who befriended the awkward misfits, who embraced the outcasts, and who bridged the distance between a "them" and an "us."

"Jonny was the first friend I made at BU, and though we've fallen out of touch over the years, I'll always remember him as the happiest, friendliest kid I ever met there. Rest in peace old friend," wrote one of Jonny's college friends on his Facebook page after he died.

"Shocked to hear the terrible news on the passing of Jonny Rose," wrote another friend. "He was one of my first friends I made out here in California and simply one of the kindest hearts I have ever come across."

He was loved, and he loved. I loved him. He was a big brother, and you always assume that your big brother will be in your life well after your parents die, a perpetual pain-in-the-ass who will drive you crazy.

My world will never be the same. I do not even know if I am a sibling anymore. When new acquaintances ask me if I have any brothers or sisters, I say that I do not, but all of it feels fraudulent somehow, like this is not my life.

I guess that is what traveling through the liminal space feels like for everyone. The part of your life that made sense is over, and you have to move to a new place that makes sense again. Until you get there, it is going to feel awkward and surreal. When you travel through the liminal space, you have to take those things from your past that you loved, and you have to piece together a new way to improve upon them. You have to figure out how to move forward with a better and stronger set of rituals.

Eventually, you have to stop crying and make way for happiness to appear.

I have to figure out how to roll with it, you know? I was at work one day, and everything was okay, and the next moment, my brother was dead, and nothing was okay.

But honestly, that is just life. It is part of the human condition. We all get dropped to our knees by something unexpected. Your brother dies. You lose your job, or your husband cheats on you.

Or some 23-year-old millennial says "fuck" at a funeral. You have to figure it out, and eventually, you have to stop crying.

That is why I said what I said at my dead brother's funeral. I told a few stories, and then I looked down. I decided that even if it embarrassed my dad, I was going to say what needed to be said. I looked up, and I looked down again.

Then I decided to go for it. I looked up at my dad again, and I grinned. He gave me a look that said, "Don't you dare."

But I dared.

"My dad is going to kill me for saying this," I said, watching my dad cringe, "but this is what Jonny would tell you if he were here: 'Stop crying, you bunch of fucking pussies.'"

CHAPTER 6
HOCKEY
TONY

I want to paint a picture of Jonny at his best: Jonny was slim and strong and athletically inclined. He was gregarious and charming and rich with friends. Throughout his life, Jonny gave our family an identity. We were a "hockey family," which we never would have been absent Jonny.

As a child, Jonny played Little League and soccer, but his true love was ice hockey. He begged me for lessons. The trouble was that ice hockey lessons started in the early mornings, and I was unwilling to awaken at ungodly hours on weekends. When Jonny had enough of Little League and soccer, I compromised by signing him up for roller hockey. The practices were held at a sane hour of the day, and he could learn to skate. Jonny spent a fair amount of time in the parking lot of Studio City Park (now Beeman) playing roller hockey with people who would go on to become lifelong friends.

But Jonny persisted in his demands to play ice hockey, and he finally prevailed. At the age of ten, Jonny became a Golden Bear, where he practiced ice hockey at 5:30 a.m. at Pickwick, a skating rink in Burbank, which was just a fifteen-minute drive from our home. Hockey became Jonny's life. He knew from the get-go that he would be valuable on the ice, and he was. When he was fourteen, he joined the Los Angeles Jr. Kings Program, a travel hockey team that not only practiced at ungodly hours but also practiced in a rink near Los Angeles International Airport. Three or four times a week, I was making the 45-minute trek to drive Jonny to his ice hockey practice.

Jonny also had weekend tournaments in other cities with games that began at equally ridiculous hours.

Soon, though, hockey became my life as well—at least my family life. One weekend a month, we would awaken before the sun rose to drive to tournaments. Thanksgivings were spent at sketchy motels where the entire family would eat canned turkey so that we could be together for Jonny's game. We even bought season tickets to the Los Angeles Kings.

Thanks to Jonny, we became a hockey family, adopting all of the associated rituals and traditions. We still are a hockey family. We attend the Kings games now in Jonny's honor, but we have grown to love the game almost as much as Jonny did. Jonny, hockey, and the Rose family: These things walk hand-in-hand.

As a high school student, Jonny was a AA-rated player, and he was almost good enough to be AAA, which is close to the highest competitive tier for youth hockey players. He was resourceful and scrappy on the ice, and I felt proud to introduce myself as "Jon Rose's dad." On the ice, Jonny appeared to be the kind of person who would grow into a man I would respect.

As much as I initially resisted the early morning hours, in the end, I loved driving Jonny around. It felt important. Certainly, my own dad never spent as much time with me as I did with Jonny, so it became something that was healing. I was fixing something broken inside of me by doing it right. On those long drives to and from games and practices, I got to know my son. Often, his friends would ride beside him, laughing and telling stories about their lives. I would listen from the driver's seat, occasionally interjecting with a joke.

When he was a junior in high school, Jonny had a tournament in Las Vegas. The night before one of his games, I won five or six thousand dollars playing craps. I have never gambled for big money, so winning that amount of money was a once-in-a-lifetime experience for me. In the morning, on the way to the tournament, I was still celebrating, and I decided to share my good fortune.

"I won some money last night," I said over my shoulder on the ride to the rink. Jonny and Alex sat in the back seat, well-rested and ready for the big day. They were awkward, pubescent boys whose gear stunk and whose voices had not yet changed. They were just babies in the backseat of a car who had no concerns other than the hockey tournament ahead of them.

Then, I shocked them by throwing several hundred-dollar bills into the back seat.

"Here," I said. "Have some money!"

I did it as much to shock them as to make them laugh—to watch my son shake in laughter as he and Alex scrambled to grab at those hundred-dollar bills.

If you have children, you know that it is not enough that they are "okay." You want them to holler in delight. You will do almost anything to see an expression of pure joy on your child's face, including tossing hundred-dollar bills into the back seat of a car. We are programmed, I think, to manifest this in our children.

After Jonny died, his friend and teammate Alex said to me, "Tony, you were one of the guys." I took that to mean that they were comfortable being around me. Thinking of this fills me up. It was what I had hoped—to be bonded to my son. I was given this gift because of ice hockey, because Jonny insisted on those early morning practices at an ungodly hour.

Now I want to paint another picture: Jonny was spoiled, and when it came time for him to transition from child to man, he was unable to take that journey. He remained stuck in the liminal space, no longer granted the forgiveness we award to young people but unwilling to assume the responsibility we expect of adults. In some ways, I believe that I ruined him.

Did I say "no" to my son often enough? I do not think I did. Instead, I threw money at him. Desperate to see that look of joy on his face, I did what Jonny wanted me to do. When he ordered a kegerator on my credit card, I paid the bill. After all, boys will be boys. When he charged meals on my credit card, I lectured him, but I did not take the credit card away. I was, as you recall, the guy who threw hundred-dollar bills at his pubescent son.

For a while, Jonny seemed to be thriving. He got good grades, excelled as a hockey player, and he was popular. When Jonny went to Boston University, he made friends instantly through the intramural roller hockey and, later, ice hockey teams. Immediately, two seniors invited him to move out of the freshman dorm and into their apartment off-campus.

While he was a junior at BU, Jonny's ice hockey club team won the Beanpot, which is an ice hockey tournament amongst Boston's four major college hockey schools—Boston University, Boston College, Harvard, and Northeastern. At the celebratory party, he met Lauren, a hockey player for the Boston College Lady Eagles. Lauren would become Jonny's girlfriend for seven years during and after college. The following year, BU played against Boston College on College's ice. The Boston College Lady Eagles, including Lauren, came holding signs—for Jonny.

In those moments, it was an honor to be Jonathan Thomas Rose's father. It is easy to be happy when the sun is smiling down on you—when your healthy newborn son's eyes are locked onto yours, when he smiles at you from the rink after winning a hockey tournament, or when he tells you that he has fallen in love.

It is harder to be happy when you know that you have failed your son. And in the years after he graduated school, he began to fall apart. I was even ashamed of him. For now, I will allow you to sit without detail because for now, the details are not important. What is important is this: Before he died, I was ashamed of my son. Before my phone rang, while I was in Bandon Dunes golfing with Jeffrey Lauterbach, I knew that I had a mess on my hands and that when I returned home, I would have to deal with the seeming failure of my son.

•   •   •

I tell you this because I have lived on both sides of the coin—I have wanted to deify my son, and I have felt regret for whom I turned my son into. Even as I honor his life and memory, I feel sadness over the failures I see in my ability to parent him effectively.

And as I talk to other people who have lost loved ones, I see them struggle to find this balance. There are those who feel such regret that they take down every picture, refuse to speak of their deceased loved ones, and create taboos on what can and cannot be discussed. As a result, they never have an honest, realistic discussion of who that person was and what lessons could be taken from his or her life.

And there are those who worship their deceased loved ones. They create shrines in their memory, and they begin to worship a graven idol. This edification can take up so much room that they have no room left to be inspired by others. They are stuck on a moment.

The thing about a person is that they are both a hero and a failure. Just as an empty chair can assume importance beyond that which it is, so can the elevated memory of a person. The memories you carry of your loved one can become so romanticized that you are unable to see other moments or other people worthy of inspiring you.

On the other hand, you can fixate so much on the lost opportunities that your regret explodes. It can take over your presence such that you do not grow from the lessons.

It is as the old adage goes: Failure is not the opposite of success. It is part of success. Your ability to succeed now, in the context of your new life, requires that you acknowledge your loved one's failures as much as their successes.

The balance comes when you can see that the hero and the failure can coexist, that you need not romanticize a person so much that no one else is worthy, nor must you live in regret. Instead, you can take the lessons from the person's life to move forward toward a future informed but not shackled by the teachings of your past.

CHAPTER 7
THE BITCHES THAT COME ROLLING IN
KATIE

It was both the worse day of my life and the best day of my life—the day that Jonny died. I have never felt more love than I did on July 27, 2015. After my mom's call, the day was a blur, but this I remember: Everyone appeared for me. I bet they appeared for you too—if you let them. People have a way of doing that. Even the people with whom you have troubled relationships will drop everything to sit by you when the hour is dark. Oftentimes, you will find that even acquaintances, people who are barely more than strangers, will sit with you.

Death has a way of bringing out the best in people. They drop everything else—the grievances, the anger, the resentments—and they give you pure love.

After Jonny died, everyone arrived in a blink: my friends, my dad's colleagues, my mom's friends, Jonny's friends, and his girlfriend. One of my friends, Erica, was a six-hour drive away, and she magically appeared at my doorstep within four hours of learning about Jonny's death. I do not know how that happened, but I do know this: Even though traffic will not be on your side when your brother dies, your friends will be there—tenfold.

A few weeks after Jonny died, my dad went on an annual fishing trip to Fort Smith, Montana. He considered canceling the trip, but my mom and I insisted that he go. To hear him tell of the love that his friends showered down upon him brought tears to my eyes. One of the men on the trip, Kenny Stavert, is an opera singer, and on the last night of the trip, nestled in a canyon, Kenny sang an opera piece for my dad. His voice, powerful on any day, reverberated through the canyon so that all of the hundreds of people living in the Fort Smith area heard the song for my dad. It was a song of fellowship, and my dad cannot describe it without finding himself stopped by tears. It was nothing short of palliative for a man who should not have seen his son's life all the way to death.

I think you will find comfort, and perhaps even a few life lessons, in remembering what happened and who sat beside you when your world fell apart. Who were the Kenny Staverts and the Ericas who arrived for you? If you pay attention to who they were and how you felt, I think you will see that this feeling of connectivity, of love, and of compassion is something you want every day.

The Rose family friends sat in a circle of chairs in my driveway. We drank wine, and we smoked cigarettes, and we laughed and cried and shared stories about my brother. We were waiting for my dad, who had been in another state when Jonny died.

I remember thinking that once he arrived, our family would be as complete as it would ever be again.

Over and over again, we asked, "What happened?"

Maybe Jonny was thinking the same thing: *Damn, damn, damn. How the hell did this happen?* Perhaps he was hovering above us, wearing the same look as he had when I first saw him after his seizure—a mixture of disheveled, baffled, and defeated. *Damn, damn, damn. How the hell did this happen?*

One way or another, however the hell it happened, the love that I felt while I sat there was unmistakable. I bet you know what I am describing.

As my friend Krystal was leaving, she hugged my mom. I do not know what Krystal whispered in my mom's ear, but my tiny little mom stood back, surveyed the gathering, and announced: "This bitch can come rolling through any day!"

"This bitch can come rolling through any day!"

Those were the words my 65-year-old mom, torn with grief, said to a twenty-something-year-old in her driveway, just hours after finding her first-born dead. We all burst into laughter in that absurd, surreal way that laughter can shine through grief.

Everything was forgiven in that minute. Every problem I had with any of my friends, with my mother, with Jonny's friends, and even with Jonny—every problem fell away. Everyone forgave me, and I forgave them. We were all in it together, sharing the pain, letting go of everything else, and grasping for happiness, love, comfort, and support wherever we could find it.

And that is what I think is important for you to remember. When our worlds fall apart, we naturally crave happiness, love, comfort, and support. In whatever way that we can, we want reprieve from the pain—happiness, in whatever way we can get it. And when we see someone else in a state of despair, we naturally provide comfort, love, and forgiveness.

There are lessons in that. Here is one: Is the way that you are reaching for happiness working? Is it fucking working? Because if it is not working, look back on what did work in your darkest hours, and do that. I believe that in our darkest hours, in times of great despair, we naturally do and give to others what works. We give love, laughter, forgiveness. We do not have to *ignore* the small stuff because we do not even *see* the small stuff. Petty things do not matter.

What if we reached for that same goodness all of the time, not only on the big days, but also every day? What if we decided to do more of the things that worked and fewer of the things that did not work?

Being surrounded by friends and sharing yourself with them? That worked for me. I cannot imagine getting through that day without the support from the kind souls who came and held my hand.

One of Jonny's friends got so drunk that he vomited. That was his way to still the pain. We called an Uber car to drive Jonny's friend home, and as several of us walked him to the Uber and helped him climb into the backseat, the driver said, "Wow. Looks like a hell of a party."

"You want in on this party?" I asked, suddenly feeling the anger. "My brother just died."

That moment of hostility? It did not work for me. I was trying to give my pain to someone else because I thought that if I shared my pain with a stranger, I would somehow feel better. In retrospect, I wish I had acted more compassionately. I promise that I was doing the best I could in that moment, but that Uber driver did not deserve my outburst. I bullied him. I should have been kinder. I should not have tried to give my pain to him.

When someone you love dies, your old self dies too. You are no longer a sibling or a mother of a 28-year-old son or Jonny's girlfriend. The person you once were? That is not you anymore. Your identity is different. From my vantage point, though, there are only two ways this new person can manifest. You either become a person who rises above death, or you become a person who lets it rule your life. There are good days and bad days either way, but it seems to me that in the end, there is no in between. You either decide that you are going to reach for happiness, love, and compassion in ways that work, or you decide that you are going to be wrapped up in grief, lashing out, and chaotic, reaching for happiness through external things that provide instant gratification, like drugs, which never really work in the end.

I read a quote once from an author named Josh Shipp: "You either get bitter or get better. It's that simple. You either take what has been dealt to you and allow it to make you a better person, or you allow it to tear you down. The choice does not belong to fate. It belongs to you."

If you become the person who rises above death, something magical happens: You start to see beauty where you did not notice it before. You find compassion in your own self where it was once absent. You learn what true friendships look like. You become thankful for the small wonders you would have earlier overlooked. And as you weed your way through new emotions, you find strength that you did not know you were capable of having. Your pain paves the way for tremendous appreciation. What you have lost gives a voice to what you have and what you can be. You begin to look at the moments as small treasures. You pay attention to them, and you consider how you can give your best self to every moment.

What I can learn from my own display of misdirected anger toward that Uber driver is this: Other people are in pain, and you cannot always tell from looking at them. Sometimes, what looks like a party is actually a funeral. Sometimes, what looks like a bully is actually a person in despair. We should forgive people, then, if we can. Or, at a minimum, at least we should not take their anger or rudeness so personally. We should remember that only people who feel unhappy on the inside are outwardly unkind, so we should always reach for compassion because we will never know what is happening in the background.

I am not sure I would have had this insight, and most certainly not at my age, if my brother were alive. I am trying—every day—to become a better person not just *in spite of* my brother's death but *because of* my brother's death.

It is a daily commitment, though, for sure. Right now, I am trying to reconcile my renewed commitment toward compassion with an increased lack of patience. On the one hand, I am so much more understanding and forgiving of other people's flaws. If someone says something unkind, I have sympathy because I have no idea what is happening or has happened in that person's life. Beyond that, being hostile or unforgiving is a waste of my time. It eats me up. But on the other hand, I am so obviously less patient with other people's petty grievances. My brother died, so I find it hard to listen to people's day-to-day complaints. A friend of mine broke his wrist and spent six weeks complaining about it. People are dying all around him, and he was upset because his wrist was temporarily in a cast.

I do not know how to reconcile those two things anymore. It seems like I may never be able to relate to people who have not felt great pain. This can be frustrating, and, at times, I find myself feeling distant and removed from people who cannot see the magnitude of pain that exists.

In the days following the Las Vegas shooting at Mandalay Bay, I was almost unable to unfold from the grief. A friend of mine complained about losing a few hundred dollars, and I could barely speak. Mothers lost their children. People's spouses died in their arms. And I knew that in the days and the months to come, those people would feel more agony than they had felt in their entire lives. My ability to relate to their pain was at the expense of my ability to relate to ordinary people having ordinary life experiences.

That is the paradox I am trying to solve today: I am more connected to pain. I am less connected to day-to-day-ness. Just when I start to get sucked into the impatience and frustration, though, I remind myself that it is the small things that make up a day. Rarely do the big events occur, but we can always reach for the best of ourselves by taking advantage of the small opportunities to provide love and compassion, letting all of the grievances fall away. We have to remember that in whatever way that pain exists, we have to all be in it together, sharing the pain, forgiving each other, and looking for those tiny little moments of joy when some little old woman says that a "bitch" can come "rolling through any day."

CHAPTER 8
SUNDRY
TONY

Here is something that might sound exceptionally resilient: There was once a world in which Jonathan Thomas Rose never existed, and Chris and I were fine. There was a time when it was just Chris and me. We had not yet been born as parents, not yet crossed through that liminal space of being a couple that transitioned first into a family of three and then into a family of four. And yet, we were already people.

And so, on my best days (and there are becoming more and more of them), I can envision myself traveling through the Twilight Zone of liminal spaces into a new future, one in which I feel blessed to have been given the extraordinary gift of knowing Jonathan Thomas Rose for 28 years, 10 months, and 29 days before his time expired, and one in which I speak of him often and fondly, with the knowledge that I have the honor of bearing witness to a person's entire life.

Theoretically, I know that I must choose happiness. In the words of Leo Tolstoy, "If you want to be happy, be."

I must choose to believe that my future will be happy, even in the context of Jonny being absent from it. I said earlier that it is easy to choose happiness when the sun is shining on you. In times of extreme grief, this choice of happiness is its most critical, and it is when I am most committed and when I know the effort must be daily or even hourly.

I believe that to be true. Yet, there are two other things you should know that are also true. The first is this: When I walk into his room, you cannot think that I don't look at his picture and say, "What the hell happened, Jonny?"

That is the question that will never be answered. How did we end up here? Jonny was an "is," and now he is a "was." Remember when I said that I had wanted to tell everyone that my son died? This was because, in the flash of an eye, as I traveled on an airplane from North Bend to Portland to Los Angeles International, I had to stop talking about Jonny in the present tense. I had to stop talking about his current love of hockey, his infectious laugh, and his rich and committed group of friends. I had to put all of that into the past tense. I had to say, "My son *loved* hockey. My son *had* an infectious laugh, and my son *had* a rich and committed group of friends."

I also had to stop ruminating about his tortured emotional last years of life.

It has taken me three years to transition from the entrance into that liminal space into the person I am today—and I was trying to accomplish it on a ten-hour plane ride from North Bend to Los Angeles. Between now and then, plenty of bad moments have won. I am certain I will succumb to others. I will lament the unfairness of a father losing his son too soon—of a child dying before the parents he created.

A gaping hole sits in my heart, and that informs every part of my thinking, my community, and my identity. I saw Jonny's entire life. It is a cruel trick on a parent, to allow them to see their child's entire life.

Here is the second thing you should know: I felt relief when Jonny died.

Is that not abhorrent? And yet, it is true. When my own son died, I felt relief.

In the years and months before Jonny died, I had been in a state of despair for Jonny, and I knew that I was facing uphill battles in my efforts to parent him. On that golfing trip with Jeffrey Lauterbach, I had come to the conclusion that when I returned home, I would finally have some difficult conversations with Jonny. (Or, at least, I was humoring myself by saying that I would have these conversations.) He needed to move out. He needed to get a job—any job, even if it was a minimum-wage-paying job that did not use his law school degree or his law license. Absent this, we would not support him financially. He also needed to take care of his body and his health. He was shoveling fast food down his mouth as fast as he could, drinking beer, and sleeping until noon. I knew he was taking drugs. He was not working, and Chris and I were paying for everything. I simply could not have him living in our home if he continued with his lifestyle.

You must ask: Why had I not had these conversations before? The truth is that it had been too inconvenient for me to take all the actions I needed to take with Jonny. Chris and I had sought a life of convenience, so instead of picking the battles, we went to bed. Instead of kicking Jonny out, we rolled our eyes and went about our business. As much as people say that we are now courageous in our ability to move forward after our son's death, Chris and I were cowardly when it came to drawing lines and taking the hard road.

On that day that Chris called, though, and in the days that came before it, I knew that I needed to do something courageous: I needed to parent my son. When I returned from my trip, I needed to implement the tough love that he so desperately needed, even if it pained me and was late in coming. I had to say words that I knew would inflict short-term pain on him and on myself, and I had to pray that those words would make a long-term positive impact. I had to take a giant, painful leap of faith and draw some boundaries with my own son. Better late than never, I told myself.

Jonny's life and the trajectory he was on were careening me toward having to do and be and say things I did not *want* to do or be or say—but *should have* done and been and said long ago. I had to be a better parent, and I was at the point of losing patience with Jonny's angst.

Jonny was terribly smart. I say "terribly" because the easiness with which he learned material was not necessarily a blessing. He skated through his four years of undergraduate school, and by the time he made it to law school, he had accumulated years and years of experience in putting in minimum effort for maximum results.

As a result, he vastly underestimated what was necessary to succeed in law school. Though I believe he was fully capable, and he even helped tutor his classmates, his grades were poor. Law school kicked him in the rear end. His undergraduate career, though not remarkable, was still successful. He did not have to work hard to still graduate *cum laude*.

Law school was another matter entirely. The shortcuts and tricks he had used for undergrad did not work in the more demanding environment of law school. Based on the entire experience of his life to date, he thought law school would be easy; instead, he was on the verge of academic probation.

Through it all, he complained: It was always someone else's fault. He helped other students with their homework, so he did not have time for his own studies, he said, adding that his professors screwed him over. His life and his tough breaks were always the byproduct of what someone or something else was doing to him.

The angst over small obstacles was shocking, and I had a difficult time respecting him as a man. He found it easier to complain than to change, so he complained.

When he was in his first year of law school, Jonny failed to turn a paper in on time. The friend he was helping, on the other hand, did manage to get her paper done. It's hard to explain his response to what seemed to me to be a minor life obstacle. It seemed to me that the solution was simple: Own the mistake, grow from it, and recover in the best way possible. This was basic failure recovery: We move past our mistakes best when we learn lessons and grow from them.

This is not what Jonny did. He panicked and became despondent. He could not physically walk into the professor's office and turn in the paper. Instead, my then 25-year-old son called me, his father, to meet him on campus. I will admit that driving to his law school campus and meeting my adult son so that he could turn in a damn paper felt awful. It was not something that I could or can make sense of.

When I found him, Jonny's face was swollen. His eyes were red, and he was shaking. I am not sure what story he had told himself that made him believe his life was over, but I was scared that Jonny's despondency was leading him toward considering suicide. He needed someone to be with him so that he could turn the paper in without falling apart. I did not know what to do, so I stood with my son, I gave him a pep talk, and I watched him walk his overdue paper into his professor's office.

That kid who had been thriving—who had earned good grades at Boston University, who had won the Beanpot, who had charmed so many people—had turned into someone I did not understand. By the time he died, Jonny was a 28-year-old man living in his parents' pool house. He was unemployed. Chris and I were paying for Jonny's therapy, but nonetheless, he rolled out of bed at about noon each day, if he felt like it. Jonny spent the day disheveled, unshowered, and angst-ridden. He spent the evenings with friends, making them laugh and helping them sort through their own lives, never sorting through his own.

There is a lot I should have done differently. I was far more permissive than what would have been good for him. Chris and I should have been willing to pay the emotional price of saying "no" to our son. We should have required him to stand up, take responsibility, and be a grown-up. We should have cut him off financially at the age of 22. We should have kicked him out of the house and forced him to find a way to take care of himself. We should never have allowed him to treat Katie the way he treated her. We should have said, "grow up," and we should have meant it. We should have said, "Your angst and blame are unacceptable, and I do not care what it takes, but you need to fix yourself."

The short-term pain of kicking my own son out of my house was unbearable. The short-term pain of enforcing consequences was not something I wanted to do. By the time he died, I was a father in despair.

In May of 2013, I wrote him a letter.

Son,

My heart is so heavy that you seem burdened and unsettled. I imagine that the life you are leading is not the one that you imagined when you were younger. Maybe things were too easy when you were younger or maybe too hard. It is hard for me to tell. One thing I know is that the world rests heavy on your shoulders.

If I have failed to be a comfort to you, forgive my inability to be there for you in the way you need me to be. I regret not being able to help you with this burden more than I have. As you realize, this is something you have to work through yourself. Tell me the way you would like me to support you, and I will be there. What I can do is support and root for you. I always have. I love you more than you know.

You have seemed to me to be always a competitive sort. Your view of yourself is through the prism of what others think about you.

You have found, I am sure, that you fail to live up to any standards you imagine others have toward you. That is not unusual. I think that all of us disappoint others. They can't imagine what we think and feel, really, and they never can understand why we act the way we do. We ultimately live our own lives, and any judgments people put to our lives are usually wrong. It is what we think of ourselves that really counts. I worry that the standards you place upon yourself feature the negative and discount the positives of what you have accomplished in your life thus far. Compete with yourself, but do it in a way that does not expect perfection. Just expect progress, a little every day. A little progress with every experience is the way to sustainable growth.

When you measure yourself against others, you can choose the wrong examples, and it basically never works well. I can see that you have accomplished so much. Can you see and appreciate what you are? You are a kind and passionate person who people have always wanted to be around because of your generosity of spirit.

You are intelligent and a good learner. I sensed you were successful at Apple but did not share their values. You certainly seem to be leveling at school and are successful in the Advocate program. This tells me that you have a great positive future.

You will be on a career course very different than mine, but you can be every bit as satisfied and happy about your career as me so long as you work your passion.

Jon—please think better of yourself than you do. You are far better than you give yourself credit for. Sure, there are things you can work on to improve yourself. You can work on those things as well. Just know that you start from a base of perfection. You are a perfect individual, and that is where you must start. Don't start with a view of you being critically flawed. That is simply not the case. Do not be afraid to calmly demand the respect you deserve from anyone. Don't be rude or hysterical. Just calmly expect it. If individuals fail to show you that respect, count it not as your failing but the failing of relationship. Relationship is a role you play, not who you are. Some relationships just plain don't work. You are perfect for you. The roles and relationships you play may not be perfect for you. That just means there are other relationships and roles that ARE perfect for you. I know it is hard, but you have to be patient.

Please continue to search for the right combination of roles and relationships. Don't conclude that you are the defect when things don't go right. Every negative presents a learning opportunity for you, which, if you think about it, will make you wiser and better. You will see. Don't give up on yourself. I will never give up on you because I love you and value you as a person.

I write this long note to you because we really don't have a chance to share as deeply as I would like, and this gives me an opportunity to tell you what I am really thinking. If you want to talk about it with me, I will cherish that discussion. If you just want to let it go, that is ok too.

Dad

P.S. Also, I challenge you to start doing some positive thinking about yourself.

One of the most important thing I have found is that you have to create your own measuring sticks for your success. It is most important for you to take stock of your assets. Not what everyone else thinks about you, but what you think about you. Take a half hour and write down everything that is positive about you. There is a bunch, and I am interested to know if you can see it. Write it down. It will reinforce your true value. I am happy to compare my notes to yours if you like. Write down your blessings. You have a bunch. When you step back, you will find that you have a bunch going for you.

I do not recall whether I ever gave Jonny that letter. Certainly, we never spoke of it. We never compared notes. We never had that discussion that I promised I would cherish.

The wonderful thing about Jonny's death, if there was a wonderful thing, was that I realized that I did not have to parent him any longer. I did not have to rewind and undo my parenting mistakes. I could stop writing letters to Jonny and giving him long and glorious speeches trying to prop him up.

I can just be done with it. And that comes with a certain amount of relief. The problem of Jonny is no longer a problem I need to solve.

• • •

When I say to you that I am choosing happiness, that I can climb through the Twilight Zone of liminal spaces to embrace a future without Jonny, know that I also feel relief.

Like I said earlier, the thing about a person is that they are both a hero and a failure. I am both a father who was blessed to know Jonny and who can be exceptionally resilient, and I am a father who feels relief that he does not have to fix his past failures. I am courageous, and I am a coward. I have a hole in my soul that will never close. I will always feel my love for Jonny. I will always know his great talents and feel some of his huge burden. And, at the same time, I will be thankful that I do not have to go through the journey of "fixing Jonny." Somehow, all of these statements are true.

Like Katie said, you cannot put a person in a box. Try as you will to romanticize someone, or to paint them as angelic, but no one is ever as simple as we make them out to be. Not Jonny. Not me. And not you, either.

You are a person, and as such, you cannot be perfectly reconciled, accounted for as line items on a profit-and-loss statement. Just as you must exist in the context of a loved one's death, you must also exist in the context of you as imperfect, at times chaotic, and as both a hero and a failure. Perhaps in understanding that this is true of all of us—of me, of you, of Jonny, and of the person you loved—you can move on without dwelling on what was. The victory is in the movement.

CHAPTER 9
THE BRIDGE
KATIE

There is a famous quote from the French author Antoine de Saint-Exupéry: *"Ce qui sauve, c'est de faire un pas. Encore un pas. C'est toujours le même pas que l'on recommence."* Translated to English: "What saves a man is to take a step. Then another step. It is always the same step, but you have to take it."

I interpret this to mean not that every person must take the same *actions*, but rather, this: Should you want to be saved, your path is always forward, looking toward the future, as opposed to backward, ruminating on the past.

Like my dad says, your transition out of the liminal space begins when you are able to envision a future that exists without your deceased loved one.

To get there, you must take a step. And then another step. It is always the same step, but you have to take it. These steps take you from the side of the bridge when you are thrown into chaos to the side when you begin to see the future. When you can eagerly await Thanksgiving celebrations, when you are excited about a wedding, when you can begin to make plans for your future, you are beginning your journey out of the liminal space.

Have you started to take those steps? Is it too much to ask to take just one? I think that it is not. Just as death is part of life, so too is joy. So is wild abandon. So is ecstasy.

How do you take it? This journey across the bridge—this first step? The journey exists inside of you. It begins when you give yourself permission to feel better, to accept your imperfections, to forgive the flaws in others, and to reach for the moments.

"You do not need to leave your room," wrote Franz Kafka. "Remain sitting at your table and listen. Do not even listen, simply wait, be quiet, still, and solitary. The world will freely offer itself to you to be unmasked, it has no choice, it will roll in ecstasy at your feet."

CHAPTER 10

TEN MINUTES

TONY

How do you get through it?

It is natural for others to ask me that question—especially parents. Nothing quite compares to losing a child. People who have not experienced it can try to imagine the pain, and they do try, but they cannot come close to imagining how we feel.

Sometimes, I find myself playing the "what if" game. What if he had died at the age of 10? Would my grief have been worse? What if he had died in utero, as Liz's baby did? Would my grief be like Liz's grief—so filled with *what ifs* and unseen milestones that it is unrelenting? What if Jonny had died at age 45? Would my grief have been less?

What if this was the best-case death scenario: That I benefited by having seen Jonny live almost 29 years, passing the bar, playing hockey, excelling on the ice, growing a huge network of friends?

I cannot know. What I do know is that my pain is unlike anything I have ever felt.

"I cannot imagine what you are going through," people say, rightfully so. "How do you get through something like this?"

My answer to them, and to you, is this: You never get through it. You are never not in it. It will never be okay in the way that I was okay before Jonny died. I will have a hole in my heart forever. If you are reading this, thinking of your own grief, know this: I have never met someone who has lost a child who does not have that hole. The hole is part of my being now, essential to who I am as a human. I am someone who will forever be colored by the death of my son. I will forever miss my son. I will forever feel longing for the experience I had wanted but did not have time to share with him. The hope that I might someday look at my adult son as an equal is now stripped of me.

The hole that you feel? It will never go away. It is a void that cannot be filled, a scar that will not fade.

Asking how to get through it, then, is irrelevant. It implies that you will "get over" this loss. To be certain, you will not.

How can you live your life with joy, knowing that you will forever be "in it"? That is a question that *is* relevant and that you *should* ask.

My answer is this: Chris, Katie, and I—as well as all of Jonny's friends and loved ones—have to look at our lives outside of the context of Jon as alive. We must moment stack without Jonny. If we want to move forward, we have no choice. We do not know what life could have been like had he lived, so we need to not project. It is a fruitless inanity. There is no context other than the one that includes Jon's death. It is not real.

My personal trainer recently asked me how old Jonny would have been, and I found myself surprisingly angry. Jonny would have been 28 years, 10 months, and 29 days. There is no world in which Jonny would have been any older than 28 years, 10 months, and 29 days. Jonny is dead, and so he would not ever have lived to be more than this age.

This is what it means to be forever "in it." There is no fixing the facts. They are what they are, and it is a pointless exercise to pretend like anything would or could have been anything different. This might sound harsh, but it drives the point home: There is no way to get over this, and I must not try to do so. Instead, I must try to live my life with joy, even as I am "in it."

How I go about doing that—and how you do it—is personal. There is no right or wrong way, so long as your way moves you toward joy. I know that others, having experienced great loss, feel tremendous comfort in imagining that their loved ones are spiritually present. It is a nice idea, and I welcome you to adopt this idea if it helps you. I allow for this possibility, but it is not one that I have adopted. Even if I did believe that Jonny's soul lingers on, it would be dishonest to say that his soul is telling me how to live. It would be dishonest of me to say that his presence would somehow make me a better person, or that I could be comforted by thoughts that his spirit lives on. I respect that Katie feels differently, and I even encourage her to continue her spiritual journey. Yet, just as you cannot put a person inside a box, you also cannot decide that one size fits all. What works for Katie does not work for me. It might not work for you, either.

Jonny was as flawed of a human being as ever anyone was, so his spirit would not give me inspiration, nor would it move me toward somehow becoming inspired to be a better man. That might be a tough pill to swallow, I know, but I cannot both romanticize my son and honestly help myself. I would be at odds, filled with cognitive dissonance. I could tell it as a story to make others feel happy.

Perhaps, reading this, you feel taken aback. But the truth is: Jonny is gone, forever. He is not coming back. I will not see him again in this life. Would I love to see him again? Of course, I would. That thought makes me want to cry, but I cannot spend my life living with the sole purpose of being able to see my son again. This is not the way I roll, nor do I recommend it for others.

My life is one without Jon around. That is the reality, and I have to do the work on myself so that I can live despite the ever-present hole that insists on moving itself toward the center of my heart from time to time.

What does that life look like?

What does that life look like?

What does that life look like?

This is the question I ask myself over and over. What does life look like without Jonny? It is never going to be the same life as the life I had when Jon was around, and I do not allow myself to imagine that as a future life.

Jonny can no longer give me inspiration. He is not around to do so. My evaluation of my relationship with him, though? It is what now inspires me. It inspires me to be more careful about my relationships in the future, especially with Katie, because I do not feel like I was careful enough in my relationship with Jonny. I was lazy, and certainly, I was not courageous.

So, as callous as it sounds, I wonder this: As I reflect on my relationship with him and am inspired by it, can my life be better now that Jon is dead? Somehow, through the great cascading of events, did Jonny's death set into motion some chain of events so that one day, I will feel joy unlike anything I have yet to experience? The answer is yes.

As inappropriate as it might sound to imagine that my son's death could somehow result in an improved life, this is what I imagine: a future without him that is nonetheless joyful. Is this something for which I can hope? Will not my life, Chris's life, and Katie's life be better if we allow ourselves the sliver of hope that our lives will improve markedly after Jonny's death—maybe even because of Jonny's death?

How can we project what life would have been like with Jonny around? He is not here, so we have no proof of life with Jonny in 2019, 2020, 2021, or beyond. I cannot know if the growth I am having would have been possible. I have much work to do on myself, and perhaps I would not have ever been moved to address these deficiencies if Jonny had not died. Perhaps I would not have lost 40 pounds. Perhaps I would have had a heart attack.

Yet, I cannot really imagine either way. Why? There simply exists no context other than the one that includes Jon's death. It is foreign, alien, and impossible to have such a life.

• • •

How can I live my life with joy, knowing that I will forever be "in it"? Sometimes, I live in ten-minute increments. The hole makes its way to the front of my chest, and I am forced to move it to my arm. I give myself ten minutes to do this. Ten minutes to grieve the loss of my son. And at the end of those ten minutes, I reassess. Do I need to recommit to another ten minutes of suffering because I am in it, or do I nonetheless commit to ten minutes of joy, knowing that the "in it" will always ride alongside the joy, reminding myself that it is not too much to ask for ten minutes of happiness, to speculate that I can find ten minutes of unadulterated joy?

CHAPTER 11
PLAYING WITH THE UNIVERSE
KATIE

Early on, as soon as I was able to see through the fog and start making choices, I decided that I would focus on the silver linings. In trying times, one of the ways to get through them is to find something to appreciate. And there always is something, even if it is as simple as noticing that your friend warmed a cup of coffee for you.

Each day, I write a list, thanking the universe for its smallest and biggest gifts. I thank the universe for Penny, my dog, waking me in the morning; for phone calls with friends; for finding a great parking spot.

For not being pregnant.

This look-for-the-silver-lining is not some groundbreaking discovery. You might even find it damn annoying at times. So do I. Sometimes, I just want to feel the pain that I have every right to feel. If someone were to tell me to look for the silver lining in those moments, I would want to cut off their arm with a butter knife.

But here is the truth: The silver linings do not really exist. They are created. You cannot find them when you do not want to find them or when you are not ready to find them. They are only there when you decide to see a future that allows your sorrow to coexist with joy. When your eyes are closed, you will never see the happiness, love, and even deep belly laughter waiting for you until you recognize that these emotions can arise in the presence of sadness.

My friend Hayley lost her dad. One day, she texted this to me: "I started to wonder if every happy experience will always be accompanied with sadness and if there is a difference between just recognizing that he is missing and choosing to suffer."

This is what I mean by recognizing that happiness and sadness can coexist. Can you see if you can find it? Can you create your own silver linings?

This is what I do: When I am making my gratitude list, I put the book *The Secret*[1] to work. I play with the universe. I thank her for things that have not yet happened, for the raise I am about to get, for the surprise text that is going to arrive the next morning from someone I have not spoken to in years, for the stranger I will meet the following week who will lift my mood.

And then I see if my experiment worked. Did the universe obey, acting on my behalf to bring into existence what was only in my imagination?

More often than not, she does. An ex-boyfriend reaches out to me to send good vibes. An elderly stranger at a coffee shop stops to tell me that I remind him of his daughter. That raise? I got it.

And I'm still not pregnant.

---

[1] Byrne, Rhonda. *The Secret*. New York : Hillsboro, Ore.: Atria Books, 2006.

My dad believed that Jonny was granted 28 years, 10 months, and 29 days of life, and while that might be true, I am not a fatalist. I do not believe that reality is pre-determined, nor that it is universal and set in stone. Our life, our reality, is shaped by our thoughts. It can sometimes—not always—be willed into existence.

Other than learning from it, we cannot do anything about the past. But our futures? We create those, either intentionally or unintentionally.

In 1842, Julius Robert von Mayer, a physician and one of the founders of thermodynamics, founded what is now known as the First Law of Thermodynamics, which is this: Energy cannot be created, nor can it be destroyed. It can only be changed from one form to another.

When my dad asks, *"How can you live your life with joy, knowing that you will forever be 'in it'?"* my answer is this: I do everything in my power to shift the energy of my future so that I can create those damn silver linings.

What about you? Are you open to a future of possibilities? Are you willing to play with the universe? To test her and to see what she gives you?

Ask her for love, for joy. Ask her to create those conditions for a surprising side-aching fit of laughter. And then see what she gives you.

CHAPTER 12
I DON'T FUCK WITH YOU
KATIE

If you take stock of the people you know who have lost loved ones, you will come to realize that most people deal with grief in one of three ways: with matter-of-fact reason, religion, or spirituality.

None of these are right or wrong. My dad and I, for instance, have gone down two different paths, but we support each other and do not mess with each other's beliefs. My thought is that you should use whatever moves you through the liminal space faster. Can you use religion, spirituality, or reason to reach happiness? To get better?

Then use it.

Look for ways to be happy, even if other people think you are batshit crazy. What I personally believe sounds nuts to a lot of people. Yet, it does not matter. Like I said, what works for me might not work for other people. What matters is that it works for me.

Same goes with you: What works for you might not work for other people. But if it gives you a sliver of hope, then use it, and stop worrying about what other people say you should do. Do not worry about the people who argue with you, or who tell you that you are grieving wrong, or even who think you have gone over the deep edge.

I personally have used Jonny's death as a spiritual journey, but before we get to that, let me back up.

The month before Jonny died, his higher self was guiding him to make reparations with me. We had argued about something silly—he had given my dog medication at the wrong time—and I was upset. In retrospect, it seems so trivial, one of those day-to-day frustrations that does not really matter in the grand scheme of things. Nonetheless, I brought it to his attention, and I probably did not address it as constructively as I could have.

Jonny exploded. The fight was typical. Jonny could not discuss things rationally. He could not simply resolve the conflict with a quick conversation. Instead, it was an all-out attack on my character. I was used to the beating, so, at the time, the fight was just another fight during which my brother verbally attacked me.

Then, Jonny did something shocking.

He apologized. My brother apologized. Then, he wrapped his arms around me and told me he loved me.

It was the only time I can remember Jonny telling me that he loved me, and it happened a month before he died. I had wanted that my entire life—my brother hugging me and telling me he loved me.

When I consider the timing of this, I have no doubt that Jonny's soul was preparing to die and that it was guiding him to make reparations with me in advance.

Some people might say that the timing was a coincidence. In fact, more than a few people have rolled their eyes or even told me that I am reading things into the situation that did not exist. You might even think this sounds crazy. There was a time before July 27, 2015, when I, myself, would have mocked someone like me.

Now that Jonny is dead, though, I have a different perspective. I think the naysayers should leave us all alone and let us process grief in the way that works for us, even if it's not what our parents or our friends or our spouses want us to do.

Here is what I believe and what makes me feel happier: On that day that Jonny showed me the uncharacteristic act of love, something inside of him prompted him to make amends. He told me that he loved me because his soul was reaching an "exit point"—his final one.

If you have never heard of an exit point, let me explain.

After Jonny died, I started researching ways to communicate with him. I searched for mediums, psychics, spiritual healers—anyone who could provide me with comfort. During that time, I stumbled upon a medium named Thomas John. My brother, of course, was Jonathan Thomas, so I took this as a sign that I should look more into Thomas's work.

One day, while I was watching Thomas's videos, something caught my attention: the idea of exit points. Exit points happen throughout a person's life—usually four or five or six times. During these points, a person's soul is deciding to stay in the physical world or to return to its original form as a spiritual being. The soul decides what is best for itself and all the supporting souls around it. If the person's soul decides to return to the spiritual world by dying, his soul drives him—usually without his conscious knowledge—to make amends and tie up loose ends.

I believe that Jonny's seizure was the beginning of his final exit point. It was then that his higher self began informing his unconscious mind to make amends and pave the way for his transition.

My dad says that Jonny's death was not my fault or his fault or my mom's fault, and I know that is true. To imagine it as anyone's fault is to give a person so much more power than he or she has. The entire universe was working on Jonny's behalf, preparing him and everyone around him for his death. His death was so much bigger than me or Jonny or my mom or dad.

I mean, how can I not believe in a connected universe acting on behalf of all humankind when a friend writing his doctoral dissertation on the liminal space just happened to be with my dad when the liminal transition began?

I look back on Jonny's seizure as a blessing. His soul was preparing to leave his body, and Jonny was putting his affairs in order, even if he did not consciously know that he was going to transition out of this world. Those six months between his seizure and his death were Jonny's liminal space, and during that time, he made amends with me in so many ways.

Here is another example: While I was driving him to and from work, we developed, for the first time, shared experiences. We listened to songs that we both loved. One of our favorites was "I Don't Fuck with You" by Big Sean.

It was small, I know, to focus on the shared song. But in the context of what our relationship had been, it was a huge step for us to have a shared anything. I had wanted a brother who would be my friend for my entire life, and Jonny gave me a taste of that on our daily rides. It was not enough to fix everything that was broken, but it was something.

For a moment, during those car rides, I got to see my brother as the rest of the world saw him: engaging and gregarious. Though he never told me directly, he told others that he was thankful that I was willing to drive him around. During those 45 minutes on the way to and from work, I spent time with the charming man that Jonny so freely offered to the rest of the world.

A few weeks after he died, Jonny played some songs for me. You read that right. After Jonny died, he played some songs for me.

Desperate to know how Jonny died, I had hacked into his phone so that I could read his text messages and find clues that might give us answers. Had he overdosed? How many pills had he been taking, anyway? I did not think it was intentional, but I truly, truly thought he overdosed.

I did not find the answers I was looking for, but what happened instead was more meaningful—and it was fascinating. All the sudden, Jonny's phone began making unprompted screen changes. A song started, and then another song, and another. On came songs like "Celestial Beings" and "I Feel Like Dying," which shook me to the core, and songs like "Teach Me How to Dougie," which made me laugh.

I was not touching his phone, and yet, his email program launched, and someone, somehow began typing an email to Alex from Jonny's email account.

The best explanation, of course, is that his phone simply had a glitch. But here is where it got stranger: It happened to my mom's phone too, and later, to my own phone. Each time, there was a message from Jonny.

You know who it did not happen to, though? My dad. And I think that was intentional: My dad has handled Jonny's death with matter-of-fact reasoning. It works for him. He has had more personal growth in the three years since Jonny's death than he has in his entire life. Forcing my dad to consider the spiritual side of this would have messed with his own method of coping.

You might agree with my dad. You might think I'm trying to hold onto something that is gone. You might think that the psychics and psychic healers of the world are nothing short of criminals who are taking advantage of grief to make a quick buck. I give you permission to roll your eyes, inwardly or outwardly. I might have once agreed with you.

Nowadays, I wonder: What do we actually know? How could a 28-year-old die? How could a person be at once a saint and a tormentor?

And how much did anyone know about Jonny, anyway? Ten percent? Fifteen percent?

There are too many unanswered questions out there for me to feel certain about anything these days. The best I can do is to find what works for me and to move through the liminal space.

I believe that Jonny played those songs to comfort me—to tell me that everything was okay. After all, when the decision that the soul makes is to leave, should we not celebrate it? If the soul is making a decision for its higher self, should we not honor this decision? To the best of my ability, I am choosing to celebrate it—to understand that when Jonny's spirit hacks into his phone and my mom's phone and my phone, it is Jonny saying that our relationship has transitioned from existing in the physical world to existing in the spiritual world. This belief makes me a stronger, better person.

My dad will not watch the videos. They do not fit within his paradigm of Jonny's death. We coexist with two different views, both of us understanding that we are all trying to make sense of our lives and our pain—me, my mom, my dad, Ally, Lauren, Alex, Dustin, Sam, Dennis, Cash, Jake, and the many, many other people who loved Jonny. None of us is right. None of us is wrong.

No one knows anything for sure, so in my version, Jonny talked to me through his phone. (If you want video proof, just ask. I am happy to share.) Regardless, in experiencing this journey spiritually, Jonny's exit point gave me something I would never have otherwise had—a brother who showed me that he wanted the best for me.

Who is anyone else to say that didn't happen? In fact, I think we should all make this agreement: I don't fuck with you and how you process grief, and you don't fuck with me and how I process grief.

CHAPTER 13
HOW JOHNNY DIED
TONY

Jonny's autopsy report was signed by the deputy medical examiner on November 10, 2015, meaning we waited four months after his death to learn how he died. During that time, we asked all of the questions you must be asking: Was it a suicide? An accidental overdose? Did his untimely death have something to do with the seizure he had six months earlier? We could not answer these questions until the coroner's report arrived.

It was impossible to not wonder: Was there something I could have done differently?

When Chris called to tell me that she found Jonny dead, the first words out of my mouth were, "It's not your fault."

I knew, intuitively, that we would all blame ourselves in some way or another. How could we not? We certainly made mistakes as parents. We did not say "no" often enough. We were willfully blind at times, ignoring the obvious red flags that our son was dropping at our feet. We were quiet in response to his trespasses when loudness would have been a better option. When Jonny was just a baby, Chris and I separated, and I have always wondered if that separation caused early trauma that impacted Jonny's internal working model. All of these thoughts raced through my mind, even though some of them seemed absurd.

Yet, I was searching for the cause. It was as if the cause would draw boundaries around my grief. I thought that if we could explain his death, if we had answers, we would feel better. Maybe it is true that learning about the cause of a loved one's death can increase the amount of pain one experiences, but I also know that no matter what the coroner's report said, I am the only person who can be responsible for my life. It is up to me, in any circumstance, to make sure that Jonny's death informs my life in a way that is positive.

In the world of self-help and neurolinguistics programming, there is a concept called "being at cause versus being at effect."

Being at cause means that when you are in a tough situation, you ask: *What can I do to affect my world?* Being at effect means that you focus on the fact that your tough situation is the result of something outside of your control.

Here's an example: Years back, Jonny and I were driving down the 101 Freeway, which is one of the main Los Angeles thoroughfares, when I was rear-ended. Jonny's hockey bag in the trunk absorbed the blow, so Jonny and I were unhurt. My new car, which I had owned for about two weeks, however, was badly damaged.

I could focus on the jerk who rear-ended me, who gave me a false phone number and fake insurance papers. I could talk about what bad luck it was for me to have my new car in the shop within weeks of taking possession. I could be "at effect," lamenting that I was an innocent bystander at the mercy of the outside world. I could think, *How terrible for me! Why do I always get the unlucky breaks?*

I would feel powerless should I take this approach to life. I would not grow or change, but rather, I would become smaller and smaller in comparison to the big, powerful world.

Yet, if I am to be "at cause," I should ask: *What can I do to cause the results to change in the future?* I could self-reflect and realize that, when traffic builds up, I should always position my car so that there is ample room between me and the car in front of me. This way, if I am ever in danger of being rear-ended, I can move my car forward to lessen the blow. And this is what I did. I became a more diligent, prudent driver.

It might be true that I did not cause the car behind me to rear-end me, but it is also true that I am not and will never be a fully perfect human being. I have much to learn and to grow from, so why not be at cause and allow the situation to inform new, empowering behavior that allows for more control of the outcome in the future?

I try to live my life at cause. I try to identify my part of the equation and be responsible for making improvements so that I enjoy better outcomes in the future.

But there is a difference between fault and responsibility. That driving accident was the other person's *fault*. Both the driver and I, though, are *responsible* for making sure that our lives get back on track and that we grow from the experience. So, while I take responsibility for the future life I have, I will not accept fault where it doesn't belong.

It was not my fault. It was not Chris's fault. It wasn't Katie's fault or Ally's fault or Lauren's fault. None of his friends could have prevented his death. I believe that Jonny's death falls under the category of "stuff happens." Jonny's body was made only to live 28 years, 10 months, and 29 days—and then, it was set to expire.

• • •

Here is what *is* our fault and our responsibility: How we respond. What comes next. What we do with our futures. How we allow our grief and our pain to inform our character.

The scars are not our fault, but how we look at them is entirely on our shoulders. We can see them as disfiguring imperfections, or we can see them as proof that we have loved and badges of honor reminding us that we are stronger because of this love.

What's next? That lies on us.

CHAPTER 14
THE ROOM
TONY

Close to a year after Jonny's death, Katie converted the room in which he died—our pool house—into a man cave and commemorative room where we could watch hockey together. At the same time, she installed an outdoor TV on the patio adjacent to the man cave so that we could enjoy watching sports during the summer.

When Jonny died, the room held a double bed and a plastic-coated green couch that had long seen better days but that did not absorb the smell of cigarettes or cigars. It should come as no surprise that Jonny's room was a mess. He was never fastidious, and certainly the depression that he carried during the last months of his life did not motivate him to clean his environment.

Today, his hockey sticks and his diploma from Southwestern Law School hang on the wall alongside the certificate admitting him to the California State Bar. His Boston University jersey, proudly displaying the number 17—his number—hangs above a brown leather L-shaped sofa. A picture of him at his best, smiling and radiant, hangs by the door alongside a picture of Katie.

Katie situated both the man cave and patio so that we could enjoy watching hockey, football, or even the Olympics inside or out, which Jonny loved to do. The man cave is where I can smoke my cigars without interference or judgment. I love being with Katie and others, but I most enjoy the room alone. I cannot express how grateful I am to Katie that she fashioned this wonderful space that our family can use, but most of all, I am grateful to have a place to relax.

I enjoy being with the things Jon loved without having Jon's death be the dominating force.

I can see that some people might think it callous to remodel his room so close to his death. Perhaps it seems more fitting to save everything exactly as it was. Some would honor his memory by leaving the carton of cigarettes, the unmade bed, the clothes flung on the chair.

I just cannot see the beauty in this.

I am reminded of something that my friend, Felice, said a few months after Jonny died. It was a few weeks before Thanksgiving, and I was dreading the first major holiday without my son.

"Remember that Jonny does not die again on Thanksgiving," Felice said to me.

Jonny died on July 27, 2015. On that day, we began to grieve. We began processing the fact that we would never again hug him or laugh with him or share a joke with him. He died on a hot day in July.

It happened once. It will never happen again. I remind myself of this because I want to give myself permission to move forward. I want this for all of Jonny's friends and family members: Chris, Katie, Alex, Cash, Dustin, Lauren, Sam, Jake, Dennis, Ally, and his many, many friends. I do not want any of us to feel compelled to relive all of our grief, afraid to create new moments in new rooms because we are so tragically attached to the past. I want us to make new memories, discarding this notion of what was *supposed* to be, and mindful that even as we grieve, we are growing stronger. We cannot avoid living because of Jonny's passing. We can live even though Jonny died.

Jonny died, but the rest of us are still alive. We have futures. There are rooms to be lived in, lives to be changed. We have to move forward. We cannot live in the past, controlled by his memories and all of the *what ifs. What if someone had gone into Jonny's room earlier? What if he had never taken painkillers? What if we had intervened earlier? More often?*

When Katie converted the room, I felt proud of her because it was a way to keep Jonny present but not in a way that controlled us. He is still in that room, represented by his law school and hockey achievements, but the room foretells the future—the future of a family sitting on a couch watching hockey games and forming new memories.

Since Jonny's death, the door has opened and closed many times. Friends and family members have sat in the room. Katie, Chris, and I have watched games and movies together. We have filled the room with takeout and barbecue and cigars and cigarettes. After Jonny's death, his ex-girlfriend, Lauren, whom he dated for seven years during and after college, temporarily moved into his old room while she was studying to be admitted to the California State Bar.

The other night, I watched *E.T. the Extra-Terrestrial* on HBO. I watched from the television in my outdoor man cave, where I smoked a cigar and cried as E.T. touched his glowing finger to Elliott's forehead and said, "I'll be right here."

It was hard to "not go there," so I popped my head into Jonny's old room.

I could smell my dead son. Still. Three-plus years later, I could smell him in that room that has since been filled with cigars and takeout and cigarettes and so, so many people.

It was unmistakable, as I stuck my nose in his room, that Jonny's smell remains.

• • •

The moments I had with Jonny—they linger. That giant stack of memories will never be erased. But the fact that they existed—that my son's smell remains even now—should not tarnish my life. His passing made my life different. I have passed through a liminal space, whereby my rituals, my routines, and my life have changed.

But different does not mean less. My life is not the same as it was before he died. He does not have a seat at the table during holidays. I will not attend his wedding. Never will his laugh fill my ears again.

When he died, this difference felt, at first, staggering. It was as though my boat had crashed, and the ocean was tossing me around.

But as the months and years passed, and as I have crossed through the liminal space, I have realized that the differences in my life are not differences of a lesser quality. They are differences of a different quality. I have more sadness than I had before Jonny died, but my joy is deeper as well. I notice moments that I would not have noticed before Jonny died, and I notice that my feelings are becoming more pure and accessible.

Would I trade this to spend time in the company of my son? Of course, I would. But I do also hold that my memories of Jonny, and the new memories I have made since his death, are not of a lesser quality.

Differences happen. Rooms change. People we love die.

Yet, "difference" and "less" are not synonymous. Should we fall into a trap of believing that they are, we will fail to see the moments. We will be unable to see the joy and the beauty if we decide that our lives are less-than.

For me, the ocean has settled. As I look around, the view is new. It is also beautiful, rich with colors I have never seen before.

I believe the same can be true for you.

CHAPTER 15

THE SAFE PLACE

TONY

Almost a year after Jonny's death, I received a phone call from a stockbroker in the South Bay who was calling to say that he had just learned of Jonny's death. Whomever he was—and his name escapes me—he had not spoken to Jonny or any of their mutual friends in years.

Yet, he felt moved to call me and let me know how comfortable Jonny always made him feel when they were at social functions together. He said that Jonny could sense when he was feeling out of place and that Jonny would grab him, introduce him to people, and engage him in conversation.

His friends from Boston University say the same thing. More than a handful say that Jonny was the first person to include them, that he was the yarn that knitted together so many people from so many different walks of life.

Jonny graduated from Loyola High School of Los Angeles, but until the eighth grade, he attended Campbell Hall, a K-12 private school in the Studio City suburb of Los Angeles. Katie graduated from Campbell Hall five years after Jonny graduated from Loyola. Five years later, Katie attended Campbell

Hall's five-year reunion, and though he had not attended Campbell Hall for fourteen years, Jonny attended the ten-year reunion for what would have been his Campbell Hall graduating class in the same place on the same evening as Katie's five-year reunion.

For Jonny, attending the reunion of a class he didn't graduate with was a natural thing to do. He had stayed in touch with those students with whom he had attended elementary and middle school as well as the teachers. Jonny was like that: He had a wonderful ability to hold people close despite distance and time. It was normal for Jonny to attend a high school reunion for a school from which he did not graduate.

Given all of this, I have *no choice* but to believe that Jonny had a sense of people. I recognize the odd choice of words: I have no choice but to believe that Jonny had a sense of people.

What people think we are and what we actually are is oftentimes at variance. This was true of Jonny. It is true of me. And it is true of you.

We have no choice but to believe that the lore of someone is incomplete. It is not the entire story of them. Much can be said of them that is both true and untrue, depending on who is saying it.

For me, what I hold to be the truest about Jonny was exactly this: I have no choice but to believe that he had a true sense of people. He saw them, and almost as though it was genetically coded into him, he saw what they needed.

And when he could, he delivered.

For several months after Jonny's death, his ex-girlfriend, Lauren, lived in the pool house while she finished law school. When she moved out in December of 2017, my personal trainer asked me if I was happy to be done with the burden of housing a young person.

I replied that actually, we are blessed. We are blessed to be able to honor the best of Jonny by being a Safe Place. As Jonny opened his arms to all comers and made the least-accepted feel acceptable, he could have felt it as a burden. Instead, it was part of his pixie dust. He was magical with people. He built bridges between people who would have otherwise never connected. He did not just accept the flawed and the quirky; he embraced it. Perhaps, as he wrestled with his own demons, he was naturally able to reach for compassion when dealing with others.

The little complaining we do about others can be small in comparison to the huge impact we can make by being their Safe Place, by opening our arms and welcoming people. Of course, Lauren was welcome in our home, and she will always be welcome, as will so many of Jonny's friends whom we honor by taking the best of him and making it part of us.

• • •

Framed on the counter in the kitchenette of my man cave, which used to be Jonny's room, is a picture of my children from the night of the Campbell Hall reunion. Jonny has his arm around Katie. They are both smiling. They are at their best: Jonny in his element, Katie in hers, and embracing each other. I saw that not often and not nearly enough for this old man. It is this picture that I look at the most, and it reminded me that the flaws and the imperfections of a person pale in comparison to the lessons we can learn from the best of a person.

Providing a Safe Place, whether it is a room, a smile, or a conversation: This is not a bad thing to be remembered for.

CHAPTER 16
I'M STARTING TO BE OKAY
KATIE

On September 29, 2015, a few months after Jonny died, I posted this on my Facebook wall:

> I was in the middle of smiling when someone the other day questioned my sadness.
>
> They told me I did not seem upset enough over the fact that my brother just passed away. That blew my mind.
>
> How dare you question my sadness. What? Am I not allowed to smile anymore? Am I not allowed to laugh? Is the only thing I have to do is sit around and mope all day?
>
> How dare you judge me without knowing me. You don't know my daily struggles. You don't see me behind closed doors. The world I once knew has forever changed. My home feels empty, and a part of me is missing.
>
> Because I choose to continue my life doesn't mean I am any less sad than you are. I choose to see the silver lining and live every day like it is my last. If I don't, then I am just existing.

I express my sadness when I need to and go about my daily business. I smile and laugh because some days, it's the only thing that keeps me going right now. You choose to live in the trenches of this, and I choose to live on a hill.

It's simple: We all grieve differently.

My dad told me that just as he starts feeling okay, someone says, "This must be so tough," at which point he thinks: *Am I a jerk? I don't feel as bad as I used to feel. Should I feel worse?*

People come up to me, and they tell me how brave I am. They ask me how I can be okay given what has happened. They tell me that they think I am remarkable. I appreciate the sentiment, but I do not feel brave or remarkable. I feel normal. I feel as though I have no other choice.

We are all going to be brought to our knees one way or another. Death will not escape anyone. And in a sense, we are lucky for the scars it leaves, for they remind us that we should have compassion for other people's scars. Suffering the loss of a loved one means that we have loved. And it is a normal human condition.

If we want to live long and happy lives, it means that we have to live a long time. With that, inevitably, will come the death of someone close to us. We have no choice, then, but to feel pain. If we want to also live happy lives, we have no choice but to continue—to be okay, not in spite of the pain, but because of the pain.

How can you be okay because of the pain? This is what I have found: Allow the pain to wash over you, and then extract the wisdom that comes with it. Let it show you how to be more compassionate. Let it show you who your friends are. Let it show you who you want to be on the other side of this bridge you are crossing. Ask yourself what you can learn from your pain.

If you can find a way to do this, you will not just be okay; you will be better. You will be a better friend, a better spouse, a better parent, a better whatever.

There is a tendency to rate pain—to say, "Why does this person not feel more pain?" or "My pain was not as bad as yours," or, "Yes, you have it bad, but you don't have it as bad as some people."

I am guilty of this. When my friend complained about his broken wrist, I thought, "There are people dying, and you are complaining about your wrist." His pain, I told myself, did not rate as highly as mine.

My pain, though, does not rate as highly as some people's pain. The massacre in Las Vegas at Mandalay Bay that left 58 people dead, including lovers, parents, and children; the mass shooting at Pulse Nightclub that left 49 people dead; the countless school shootings; the runners whose legs were blown off minutes away from crossing the finish line as well as the spectators killed in the Boston Marathon bombing; Hurricane Katrina, with its death toll of 1,464 people; the more than 4,000 people who died in Puerto Rico during Hurricane Maria...

Those were tragedies.

My brother's death? The more I consider it, the more I begin to think that his death was not a tragedy. It was just part of life.

This brings me to the topic of how Jonny died.

I knew Jonny wasn't doing well. I knew he was taking too many painkillers and that he was drinking on top of that. I knew he had a dealer and that he was buying more pills than were being prescribed by a doctor.

It was not just the painkillers, though. I could see it. He had stopped playing hockey. He slept until noon. He would wake the rest of us up rummaging through the refrigerator at 2 a.m., drunk or high or whatever he was. He had depression and insomnia and a proclivity toward addiction.

A couple of weeks before he died, I said to my dad, "We need to do something. If we do not do something, he is going to die."

And lo and behold, he died.

I carried that guilt with me during those four months between Jonny's death and when we received the coroner's report. On the one hand, Jonny was dead just the same. Nothing could change that. He was a grown man responsible for his life, and we did the best we could at the time, given the tools and the information we had.

But could I have done more? My dad kept saying, "It's not your fault," but every time he said that, I wondered, *Do we have more responsibility in this than we think?*

I knew that my brother was going to die, and I warned my father as much. And then, my brother died.

When we finally received the coroner's report in mid-November, the first words I saw were these: "The cause of death was natural."

Jonny died of natural heart failure. He had a heart attack caused by full blockage in his left anterior descending artery. His heart stopped working, and Jonny died instantaneously. Even if my mom had found him sooner, he would have died. In fact, the informal term for the type of heart attack Jonny had is "widowmaker" because it turns spouses into widows.

Jonny didn't live to have a spouse, or children, or nieces and nephews. Sometimes, people die too young. It happens. I tell myself that my pain, albeit unbearable at times, does not rank as high as some people's pain.

I tell myself that if Jonny had died of suicide or an overdose, perhaps my pain would be worse.

Yet, this ranking of pain? It is a masturbatory exercise. What does it matter if someone has more pain than you? Or if your pain is worse than your neighbor's pain? *Should* only the person who has suffered the most—the one with the saddest, most heart-wrenching story—be allowed to grieve?

Of course not.

When you really think about it, you will start to see that rating pain is irrelevant. When you start saying that your pain is not as bad as someone else's pain, then you deny yourself the opportunity to hear the messages that your pain has to offer. When you say that your pain is greater than everyone else's pain, you exist only to have the magnitude of your pain validated by the outside world. Once again, though, if you are looking outward to make sure your pain registers higher than everyone else's pain, you are failing to extract the lessons from your grief.

We do not win awards for bearing the most pain, nor do we receive accolades for smiling through pain. And even if you could win such awards, they would barely have meaning in comparison to your grief. There is no external force waiting to wave a wand over you so that the pain ebbs or flows.

Your pain is internal. It exists inside of you. It is your pain. You cannot give it away by diminishing it in comparison to someone else's pain, nor can anyone else quiet it by showcasing their pain. You now live in the companionship of grief. It has holed up inside your heart, and it is there for a reason.

Your pain is carrying with it information. If you listen closely, it will share some of life's most beautiful secrets. It is through your deeper pain that you will find deeper compassion. It is through your sadness that you can explore the path toward joy. You will find yourself on long, dark walks, feeling broken and defeated, when you stumble across a quiet mountain lake. You will be folded in sorrow, only to find yourself being enveloped in love. You will find that pain can be your companion as you let grief release your joy. The lessons are waiting for you, asking you to grow to be old and wise, reminding you of this:

You are alive.

CHAPTER 17

17 LESSONS WE LEARNED FROM JONNY'S LIFE AND DEATH

Lesson #1: Tony

When life drops us to our knees, we believe the apocalypse has hit. Yet, it has not. Instead, we have moved to a well-traveled place called the liminal space. The liminal space is the term to describe a transition, a place of limbo. You have left one phase, one set of rituals or traditions, but you have not yet established new rituals. During the liminal stage, you are standing on the threshold between your previous way and what will become your new way. It can feel both permanent and overwhelming, and certainly so when grief accompanies it. Deep grief stems from the loss of a relationship or an extreme shift in conditions that changes the dynamic and balance in such a profound way that the circumstances of joy that persisted before the liminal phase cannot be recaptured. This loss can seem enduring. After all, how can you be okay when the joy you once had can never again be realized? Yet, the liminal space need not be permanent. You can come out of it, and you can, eventually, see a future of happiness and joy. Your pain does not need to shackle you.

Lesson #2: Katie

During those first few moments (which might be minutes, hours, or days) of being thrown into the liminal space, you will feel as though the world should stop, and yet, it continues. You will feel unable to cope, as though you are lacking the tools necessary for survival in this new world. You may find some comfort in knowing that this is normal. When the floor drops out from under you, you are supposed to feel shock. You are in a foreign land. Allow it to be.

Lesson #3: Katie

The most that you will ever know of a person is about ten or fifteen percent. When they die, you will see sides of them you never knew existed. You will learn all sorts of new information—proof that your dead brother, your dead spouse, your dead friend, or your dead child had dimensions to their personality that you never knew existed.

You will come to learn that you cannot put a person inside a box. People are too divergent, too unconstrained to be put inside a box. Try as you might, you cannot hold all of the pieces of a person in one place. They will spill out. Just when you think you have captured a person, you will notice something on the other side of the room that does not fit.

Human beings are mysterious and open for interpretation. They shift, they grow, they break. They say things they do not mean. They don't say things they wish they said. Sometimes, they hide, and sometimes, they put on a brave face. Those of us on the receiving end never really know for sure what is real, what is amplified, and what is hidden. There are too many variables.

The best we can do, then, is to allow the questions to remain unanswered and to instead make our own meaning. Absent answers to our questions, we have to interpret the past—whatever it is—in the way that best allows us to live powerfully and joyfully in the present and in the future. Since we cannot know for certain, we must do the best we can.

Lesson #4: Tony

When we allow our lives to continue, albeit very differently than we imagined, we open up the possibility of a moment of joy, which stacks onto another moment of joy, which stacks onto another moment of joy, which begins to turn not into a moment, but into a day, and then into a life.

I call this "moment stacking," and what it means is that we allow for new moments to accumulate, moments that exist without our deceased loved ones. When we pile enough of them on top of one another into a new stack of moments, we can create those new rituals. We can cross through the liminal space into a life that exists without our loved one. Our old moments still exist, but new stacks of moments have accumulated beside them.

It helps me to visualize these moment stacks as separate entities. The stack of moments that included your deceased loved one is complete. It will never be erased, but it will not have new layers. Do not allow the moments that you had in the past to be the organ that pumps into the moments that you have now.

Lesson #5: Katie

We all get dropped to our knees at some point by something unexpected. It is part of the human condition. Your brother dies. You lose your job. Your husband cheats on you. This is just life. Commit to figuring it out. Commit to taking this life, this life that no longer makes sense, and moving to a new place so that life makes sense again. Until you get there, it's going to feel awkward and surreal. Let it, and commit to rolling with it.

Lesson #6: Tony

As I talk to other people who have lost loved ones, I see them struggle to find a balance between deifying their lost one and feeling such regret and remorse that they hide. There are those who feel such regret that they take down every picture, refuse to speak of their deceased loved ones, and create taboos about what can and cannot be discussed. As a result, they never have an honest, realistic discussion of who that person was and what lessons could be taken from his or her life.

And there are those who worship their deceased loved ones. They create shrines in their memory, and they begin to worship a graven idol. This edification can take up so much room that they have no room left to be inspired by others. They are stuck on a moment.

The thing about a person is that they are both a hero and a failure. The memory of a person can become so elevated that it carries an importance beyond what it was. The memories you carry of your loved one can become so romanticized that you are unable to see other moments or other people worthy of inspiring you. On the other hand, you can fixate so much on the lost opportunities that your regret explodes. It can take over your presence in such a way that you do not grow from the lessons.

The balance comes when you can see that the hero and the failure can coexist, that you need not romanticize a person so much that no one else is worthy, nor must you live in regret. Instead, you can take the lessons from the person's life to move forward toward a future informed but not shackled by the teachings of your past.

It is as the old adage goes: Failure is not the opposite of success. It's part of success.

Lesson #7: Katie

When someone you love dies, your old self dies too. You are no longer a sibling or a mother of son or someone's girlfriend. The person you once were? That's not you anymore. Your identity is different.

From my vantage point, though, there are only two ways this new person can manifest. You either become a person who rises above death, or you become a person who lets it rule your life. There are good days and bad days either way, but it seems to me that in the end, that there is no in between. You either decide that you are going to reach for happiness, love, and compassion in ways that work, or you decide that you are going to be wrapped up in grief, lashing out and chaotic, reaching for happiness through external things that provide instant gratification, like drugs, which never really end up working in the end.

If you become the person who rises above death, something magical happens: You start to see beauty where you did not notice it before. You find compassion in your own self where it was once absent. You learn what true friendships look like. You become thankful for the small wonders you would have earlier overlooked. And as you weed your way through new emotions, you find strength that you did not know you were capable of having. Your pain paves the way for tremendous appreciation. What you have lost gives a voice to what you have and what you can be. You begin to look at the moments as small treasures. You pay attention to them, and you consider how you can give your best self to every moment.

Lesson #8: Tony

The victory is in the movement. You are a person, and as such, you cannot be perfectly reconciled, accounted for as line-items on a profit-and-loss statement. You may have moments of regret, even years of regret. In the future, you will have moments of shame, and you will have moments of great pride. Just as you must exist in the context of a loved one's death, you must also exist in the context of you as imperfect, at times chaotic, and as both a hero and a failure.

Perhaps in understanding that this is true of all of us—of me, of you, and of the person you loved—you can move on without dwelling on what you did wrong.

Lesson #9: Katie

Your transition out of the liminal space begins when you are able to envision a future that exists without your deceased loved one.

To get there, you must give yourself permission to take a step and then another step. When you can eagerly await Thanksgiving celebrations, when you are excited about a wedding, when you can begin to make plans for your future, you are beginning your journey out of the liminal space.

Have you started to take those steps? Is it too much to ask to take just one? I think that it is not. Just as death is part of life, so too is joy. So is wild abandon. So is ecstasy.

How do you take it? This journey across the bridge—this first step? The journey exists inside of you. It begins when you give yourself permission to feel better, to accept your imperfections, to forgive the flaws in others, and to reach for the moments.

Lesson #10: Katie

People will tell you to look for the silver linings, but the silver linings cannot be found; they do not really exist. They are created. You cannot find them until you decide to see a future that allows your sorrow to coexist with joy. When your eyes are closed, you will never see the happiness, love, and even deep-belly laughter waiting for you until you recognize that these emotions can arise in the presence of sadness.

Are you open to a future of possibilities? Try this: Expect the universe to deliver something small and wonderful. Ask her for it. Test her. Ask her for love, for joy. Ask her to create those conditions for a surprising side-aching fit of laughter. And then, see what she gives you.

Lesson #11: Tony

There is no changing the facts. They are what they are, and it is a pointless exercise to pretend like anything would or could have been anything different. This might sound harsh, but it drives the point home: There is no way to "get over" the death of someone you love.

Your loved one is gone, and though you would do anything to see him or her again, in this life, you will not. That might take you aback, but it must be confronted. Too often, people in grief ruminate on what life *would have been like*. But this rumination is a fruitless cycle that will take you to the same tragic ending each and every time.

Your only option, then, should you want a future of happiness, is to ask yourself *how* to move forward with joy, even in the context of your loved one's death. How can you become better, stronger, more resilient? How can you become more compassionate? What lessons can you learn from the life and death of your loved one?

This is the way to move forward.

Lesson #12: Katie

If you take stock of the people you know who have lost loved ones, you'll come to realize that most people deal with grief in one of three ways: with matter-of-fact reason, religion, or spirituality.

None of these are right or wrong. My dad and I, for instance, have gone down two different paths, but we support each other and don't mess with each other's beliefs. My thought is that you should use whatever moves you through the liminal space faster. Can you use religion, spirituality, or reason to reach happiness? To get better?

Then use it.

Look for ways to be happy, even if other people think you are doing it "wrong." What works for you might not work for other people. But if it gives you a sliver of hope, then use it, and stop worrying about what other people say you should do. Do not worry about the people who argue with you or who tell you that you are grieving wrong or even who think you have gone over the deep end.

Lesson #13: Tony

There is a difference between fault and responsibility. While it is probably not your fault that your loved one died, how you now respond is your responsibility. What comes next? What are you going to do with your future? How are you going to let your pain and your grief inform your character?

This is your responsibility.

The scars are not your fault, but how you look at them is entirely on your shoulders. You can see them as disfiguring imperfections, or you can see them as proof that you have loved and as badges of honor reminding you that you are stronger because of this love.

Lesson #14: Tony

Different is not the same as less. Your life is different. It is not the same. And these differences might feel staggering. Yet, the differences in your life do not need to be differences of a lesser quality. In my life, they are differences of a different quality. I have more sadness than I had before Jonny died, but my joy is deeper as well. I notice moments that I would not have noticed before Jonny died, and I notice that my feelings are become more pure and accessible.

Would I trade this to spend time in the company of my son? Of course I would. But I do also hold that my memories of my son, and the new memories I have made since his death, are not of a lesser quality.

Differences happen. Rooms change. People we love die.

Yet, "difference" and "less" are not synonymous. Should we fall into a trap of believing that they are, we will fail to see the moments. We will be unable to see the joy and the beauty if we decide that our lives are less-than.

For me, the waves crashing down on me have stopped, and the ocean has settled. As I look around, the view is new. It is also beautiful, rich with colors I have never seen before.

Lesson #15: Tony

The flaws and imperfections of a person pale in comparison to the lessons we can learn from the best of a person. One of the best ways to grow, then, is to take the best of your loved one. Remember who they were when they were shining. Then, go out, and be that person to the world.

Lesson #16: Katie

We have a tendency to compare pain—to say that our pain is greater than someone else's pain, or that our pain is less than someone else's pain, and that we should therefore be grateful for what we do have.

Yet, comparing pain prevents us from learning the lessons from our pain. It matters not how great our pain ranks on the scale of pain. It matters that we allow our pain to teach us lessons.

Your pain is carrying with it information. If you listen closely, it will share some of life's most beautiful secrets. It is through your deeper pain that you will find deeper compassion. It is through your sadness that you can explore the path toward joy. You will find yourself on long, dark walks, feeling broken and defeated, when you stumble across a quiet mountain lake. You will be folded in sorrow, only to find yourself being enveloped in love. You will find that pain can be your companion as you let grief release your joy. The lessons are waiting for you, asking you to grow to be old and wise, reminding you of this:

You are alive.

Lesson #17: Tony and Katie

There is no beating grief. There is no getting over it. Yet, the beauty of grief is that it stretches your emotional bandwidth. Joy, happiness, love, compassion: The extent to which you can feel them is directly proportional to the amount of pain, grief, sadness, and devastation you have felt.

While there is no beating grief, there is leveraging grief so that it increases your joy. When you do this, you see that your grief is beautiful. Embrace it.

Tribute to Jonny

This is the tribute printed on the back of the memoriam at Jonny's funeral. It is how we remember Jonny.

It seems impossible that someone so connected and anchored to the people in this world has so permanently slipped out of it. We did not hold Jon here; rather, he left parts of himself behind—and he has taken parts of us with him.

And there are so many of "us."

In the most benevolent and genuine of ways, he was the embodiment of hail-fellow-well-met. As his dear friend Alex said, Jon fit in everywhere. He left lasting impressions wherever he went, and he never failed to collect friends in his wake. If you had a hidden talent, a surprising tenderness, or a quiet sense of humor, Jon found it, and he treasured you for it.

He was smart, loving, generous, caring, and kind—the sort of person you could always bring home to meet the parents. Everyone loved Jon: His family loved him. His college friends loved him. His friends' parents loved him. Even his girlfriend's parents loved him.

And he loved us too. He was genuine in his care and concern for others. That they returned his care and concern was evident in the fact that he had the best people in his life. So many of you have called and written to express your love—so many of you who knew him deeply, and so many of you who met him only a handful of times. He saw you. He knew you. And he valued and loved you all.

About the Authors

Tony Rose is the founding partner of Rose, Snyder & Jacobs, LLP, a Los Angeles-based CPA firm that focuses on the intersection of values, knowledge, relationships, and structures that allow for wealth creation. He is the author of *Five Eyes on the Fence* and *Say Hello to the Elephants*. Tony is the proud husband of Chris and the father of Katie and Jonny (1987–2015).

Tony is lifelong student who continues developing, both professionally and personally. He is a Legacy Wealth Coach®; a Certified Kolbe Method™ Consultant; a member of the California Society of Certified Public Accountants, the American Institute of Certified Accountants, Genius Network, and Strategic Coach; a graduate of Human Interaction Technology; a guest speaker at Otis College, California Institute of the Arts, Keck School of Medicine, Hawaii

Tax Institute, and the University of Southern California Leventhal School of Accounting; the past president of the National CPA Health Care Advisors Association; and a board member for the Smith Center for Performing Arts. He has also lectured in front of civic groups and organizations of multi-generational families. Tony believes that his largest impact is not what he does as a CPA, but rather his skill as a counselor and advisor.

Tony lives in Los Angeles.

Katie Rose received her bachelor's degree in hotel administration from the University of Nevada, Las Vegas. A year later, with most of her life ahead of her, Katie's older brother, Jonny, died, sending her life and her plans into a tailspin. A loving friend and an aspiring personal coach, Katie has spent the past three years on a journey of self-awareness, reclaiming her life and her future by expanding her own capacity for compassion and resilience.

Katie lives in Los Angeles, where she works as an event planner and assists her mentor, Sean Stephenson, in spreading his wisdom. She hopes to one day coach others who are in the midst of grieving.

Katie and Tony Rose can be reached at:

www.beautifulgrief.com

Made in the USA
San Bernardino, CA
09 February 2019